D1462514

WE CANNOT FIND WORDS

The Foundations of Prayer

by

TAD DUNNE, S.J.

DIMENSION BOOKS, INC.
Denville, New Jersey 07834

You whom my heart seeks,

You the ones given,

The same,

The same!

— *from the Unwritten Biography of Euwan Mi*

FIRST ENGLISH EDITION
DIMENSION BOOKS
DENVILLE, NEW JERSEY

ISBN #0-87193-138-9

TABLE OF CONTENTS

(Dedication)

To Celia,
Craig,
Donna,
and Mary Ann

1

WHEN WE CANNOT FIND WORDS

THERE are certain passages in Scripture which, like good art, speak more profoundly to us the older we get. One of the most thought-provoking is from Paul's letter to the Romans:

> *When we cannot choose words in order to pray properly, the Spirit himself expresses our plea in a way that could never be put into words.*
> *(8:26)*

At one time or another we have all worried how to pray properly. Paul's text suggests that proper prayer still goes on when we cannot choose words, and this thought can be consoling. But over the years, we can also be filled with a series of ever-deepening reflections on the nature of prayer and on the nature of that intimacy with which God has taken up his dwelling place in our hearts.

For example, in the above passage, we might initially get the picture that during those times when we on earth are too distracted to pray, the Spirit up in heaven is interceding for us. But the more we read of St. Paul, the more we realize that this is not his picture. He sees the Spirit as doing that ineffable praying within our own consciousness, as an integral part of our busyness, our thinking things over, our being pressed with concerns. He imagines human consciousness as the bursting-out place for God's Spirit from within the womb of creation. As he says a bit earlier,

> *From the beginning till now the entire creation, as we know, has been groaning in one great act of giving birth; and not only creation, but all of us who possess the first-fruits of the Spirit, we too groan inwardly as we wait for our bodies to be set free.* (8:22-23)

Underneath our groaning, and within it, the Spirit of God himself seeks the face of God. The Spirit's prayer seems to suffuse our palpable living: times when we're busy, times when we're lost in thought, times when we are wondering what in the world is going on and what we ought to be doing about it — times, in short, when we cannot find the words to pray to God because the earth and its flesh and its blood lay their rightful claims upon our hearts.

If our efforts to be honest and unselfish about situations at hand are in fact some form of unacknowledged prayer, then why not acknowledge it? Our consciousness itself demands that we do. We are never content with an ambiguous striving for a fuller life; we also want to reflect on how this striving has God as its origin, God as its guide, and God as its endpoint. This reflection will tell us a lot about ourselves. More importantly, though, it will tell us a lot about God, particularly as being sanctifying Spirit, redeeming Word, and the loving Source of our lives. In other words, we will be able to glimpse the astonishingly intimate connection between our ability to pray and our capacity for the Trinity.

I have subtitled this little book "Foundations of Prayer." Provisionally, I am referring to the language we use to talk and think about prayer. "Foundations," in a sense, are the basic words we employ to reflect theologically about the spiritual life. It is difficult to agree on what words mean, however. We used to define prayer as "raising the mind and heart to God." And as any grade-school catechist knows, it is not easy to tell youngsters what "raising" refers to and what it does not. There are similar difficulties with the words "mind," "heart," and, perhaps most crucially, "God." So I would like to define some terms that will be useful for reflecting on every possible form of prayer, ranging from the most familiar to the most unnoticed.

The definitions, however, will be quite provisional. If I try to explain "raising" by a further definition, I may still be asked to define terms in that definition. So rather than give definitions in the ordinary sense, I intend to ask you to locate activities, or operations, within your own conscious experience to which our language will refer. I'm going to ask you to appeal to your own inner life as a Christian as the foundation of our language about prayer. The foundations of prayer, in short, will be your own personal inner history.

This procedure may seem strange at first, but I think you will find it very rewarding. You will discover, I hope, that the schoolroom of prayer is your own experience and that there are lessons there which only you can learn. You will also grow more accustomed to testing everything you read or hear about prayer against the standards of your own intelligence and conscience.

Besides revealing how the Trinity embraces our lives, and besides turning you to your own experience for prayer's foundations, these reflections will also have one very practical application. There are numerous books on prayer and numerous spiritual directors suggesting how we ought to pray. There's nothing wrong with that by itself, but many of these experts become tempted to act like storekeepers of spiritual methods: they've got the goods and we come to try them out, without much thought about what or who supplies *them* the goods in the first place. If St. Paul is right — that we pray a lot more than we realize — then we really don't need to look for new methods as much as we need to discover the kinds of prayer already going on within us.

So, rather than speak of how we ought to pray, let us look at how we do pray. In particular, let us examine the full play of human wondering. Our hope is that by understanding how our wonder works during those times when we don't think we're praying, we will come to know not only how much we do pray but — and this is the best part — who it is that lights our wonder so.

2

THE SPIRIT OF WONDER

WE begin with a series of "heart-experiments." A heart-experiment is an exercise in introspection. It aims at catching ourselves in the many ways in which we wonder and discovering how God's Spirit is active within us. But the heart is a labyrinth: it takes strange turns and can suddenly plunge one into darkness. So we must make our way slowly and carefully.

The first strange turn appears when we look at human feelings. This may sound ridiculous at first, but you and I have feelings we don't know we are having. Most of us, for example, can recall times when we discovered that we resented someone and that we had been acting out of that resentment long before we realized it. Or sometimes we can work feverishly at some project with what we think is a great sense of accomplishment, only to discover later that we were also driven by deep feelings of inadequacy. The feelings were there; they were working to shape some questions and limit others; they were guiding our attention; but at the time we didn't realize it.

Sometimes we can have immense feelings but which, like the still waters that run deep, appear motionless on the surface. I'm sure you've had the experience of getting a long-distance call from a certain town where someone you care for lives. "Detroit, Michigan, calling." And your heart, which before had no noticeable feelings about the friend there, suddenly releases a flood of powerful feelings as though the dam unexpectedly burst. It's not the constant feelings we notice; it's the changing feelings that attract our attention.

The discovery of these unnoticed but real feelings is not always an instantaneous occurrence. Take falling in love, for example. We find ourselves preoccupied with a certain person; we adjust our schedules to open up more time for him or her. We may tell ourselves that it's just a matter of good company or of sharing a common interest. But instinct may suggest something deeper.

Eventually we ask ourselves the question, Am I falling in love? We can deliberately ignore the question, but only at the cost of some honesty. If honesty brings a Yes answer to our question, then we are in the position of someone to whom something profound has happened, someone who has been motivated by a new set of forces within, but above all, someone who has come to know about it.

At this point, certainly, we can choose to withdraw from expressing that love or cooperating with it. But rather than talk about that decision I want to ask you a personal question.

Are you in love with God?

I'm asking a question of fact, and it may take time

to face the fact. You may say that you seldom feel great love for God, but I'm suggesting that you may in fact have those feelings and not realize it.

Or you may have experienced some feelings of love but not yet named them as directed towards God. You may not understand how the various drives from within you are working or where they seem to be heading. And so you may have to suspend judgment for a while. But is it really the wiser and safer path never to answer the question?

Each one of us has to answer the question alone: Am I in love with God? We can listen to the Gospel, we can listen to our parents, we can listen to our friends, we can listen to reason and logic. But none of these does the job. Whether we answer Yes or No, we put our whole selves on the line; we take responsibility for what we are to become.

Perhaps you and I already know that we are in love with God. It still takes courage to face this heart-experiment, doesn't it? This is because the answer is not a recognition of an unchanging fact; rather it's a recommitment of ourselves to continue hand-in-hand with God in whatever situation we find ourselves.

I have been talking as though being in love with God were a feeling. In fact, it might more properly be called a drive, or a force, which includes feelings, but which moves along tracks which feelings merely help direct. That drive begins in human wonder about anything and everything. The love of God asks questions, weighs answers, imagines, proposes, contemplates, worries, decides, realizes.

As you can see, I am using the word "wonder" here in its broadest sense. Although we often conjure up a picture of someone gazing in wide-eyed "wonder" at, say, the stars, we also use the word to represent painful consternation and frustration, as in "He's wondering what the hell to do next." So, by "wonder," let us mean the entire range of mental and affective movements within us which take us outside of ourselves. Getting outside of ourselves, no matter in what form, whether pleasant or painful, is the beginning of love, for love always tends outward. To examine the data on our love for God, then, let us begin by looking at some of the features of human wonder.

We notice first of all that wonder begins spontaneously insofar as questions occur to us unexpectedly and unsystematically. Wonder is not a product of creativity, it is creativity's source. It is not something we own, it is something we receive. We receive it something like the way parents receive a new-born child: as something with its own rhythms, making its own surprising demands on our attention and time and care.

Still, wonder can be stifled insofar as we refuse to follow up on the questions that occur to us. Wonder can be stifled when, for whatever reasons, we fail to reflect on ourselves or neglect to ask ourselves what we really think. Like unacknowledged feelings, our unacknowledged thoughts have an effect on our lives that is often more obvious to others than to ourselves.

Think, for example, of the way many people choose their clothes. A sixty-year-old man who wears clothes in the style of a twenty-five-year-old may deny he's worried about getting older, but nobody believes him. It's evident that he is a man who thinks a great deal about getting older but doesn't *think* that he thinks about it. His wonder about old age has been squelched in such a way that he no longer realizes that certain questions are bothering him. Fear has poisoned the very well of wonder that might have provided him insight into how he might age more graciously.

Finally, wonder itself, though it can be suppressed, has no limits in itself on its pursuit of correct understanding, decent living, and ever-deepening relationships of love. This unlimited wonder burst forth in us when we were children, and we asked more questions than our parents had either time or knowledge to answer. As adults, we know very well that we will go to our graves with unanswered questions. But we still revel in the joy — and pain — of raising questions.

It is on account of this open-ended and unlimited feature of wonder that we can say that our love for God has its roots there. Only our love for God will enable us to make ultimate sense out of everything. The relationship between all the questions we can raise about the world and the love of God is something like the relationship between a house and an unseen owner. Suppose we were to visit a house which some woman has furnished for herself. We would find that the arrangement of furniture, of colors, of art objects and utilities manifests a coherent set of ideas and purposes. We would wonder what the owner must be like, and we would have an approximate idea of what she cares about. But if we happened to meet her in person and become friends with her, then everything in her house would make a deeper sense. We would see that the order there is not only functional, it is an expression of her personality. Her house, in a sense, is *herself.*

Our world is God's house. He designed it. Not only for us to live in but for himself to live in with us. It bears the marks of his personality. Whether we realize it or not, when we wonder about its furnishings, we wonder about him. All wonder, we might say, is implicit prayer.

Conversely, all real prayer must begin in wonder. Any "prayer" that does not sprout from our wondering how things stand with us is rootless prayer. Such a "prayer," no matter how beautiful the words, no matter even how strongly felt the sentiment, when it is not spilling out of our own particular experiences of our everyday lives, counterfeits the genuine article. Wonder is the power in our prayer.

For this reason it is important to pay some attention to "distractions" in prayer. They may be the real prayer, while the words we were mumbling are really the distraction. A "distraction" will be genuine prayer insofar as it arises out of a sufficiently deep sense of wonder about something in our experience. The "prayer" may in reality be the distraction insofar as we use it to avoid facing life as it comes.

Prayer has been defined as the raising of the mind and heart to God — like a helium balloon, you might say. But we musn't let go of the string or the balloon sails away. Our prayer can lose its connection with earthly concerns and get lost in dreamy clouds of unreality. And what happens to us then? We literally fall asleep.

The usual objection to bringing daily concerns into prayer is that, compared to the love of God, they are too trivial. In a sense this is true. If, at prayer, I am worried about whether I paid the phone bill, I may have a hard time reading the Gospels. But if I let myself wonder *why* paying the phone bill worries me, then those Gospel passages that tell of God's providence speak directly to where I am. In other words, daily concerns do have a place in our prayer if we let our wonder cut into them deeply enough.

More often than not, however, I don't consider myself to be "at prayer." Throughout any given day, my mind wanders all over the place. It is sometimes curious, sometimes playful, sometimes appreciative, sometimes creative, sometimes meddlesome. How might prayer be rooted in such a variety of meanderings? Let us describe a number of them separately. At the end of each type of wonder, I will ask you to perform a heart-experiment to see how wonder naturally reaches for its God.

First we will look at examples of simple curiosity. I don't intend to claim that all curiosity necessarily ends up in prayer, but I do hope to show how it can.

Indeed, I hope to show that prayer is curiosity's natural endpoint.

A friend of mine has been very curious to know why fireflies light up. Somewhere he had heard that it has to do with mating. Recently he was out in the country at night and came across a broad, low field dotted with fireflies; their softly flashing lights seemed to communicate something of interest to one another. He noticed on the road directly in front of him two fireflies slowly crawling toward one another, their tails blinking. So he stopped to see if they were about to mate.

Unfortunately the area was thick with mosquitoes, too, thirsty ones; and they pestered him so much he couldn't wait out the slow crawl of the fireflies toward one another. He trotted out of the scene, letting what those two particular fireflies did that night remain one more of nature's countless secrets.

Neither he nor anybody else knows what happened. Perhaps they mated; perhaps they didn't. So my friend goes on wondering. Even if he were to find out why fireflies light up the way they do, he will never find out what he had once wanted to witness. They did what they did, that's all. But that's not really all. He still remembers and he still wonders.

Where does that sort of wondering head? In most cases of wondering what is so, it heads towards wondering what to do. But there are privileged moments, usually when we're traveling or taking a few days off from work, that we find ourselves wondering what is so for its own sake.

We wonder, for example, whether a tree fallen in a woods was struck by lightning or just rotted away at the base, even though finding out the answer has no practical use for us. We are creatures moving across the surface of a planet doing what no other creature we know of does: we are inquiring into what is so. It is our natural appetite.

From curiosity about individual things, our wonder can ascend to a higher curiosity about entire systems of things. That is, we can also wonder how each individual thing connects to every other thing. In this we are more like a geologist than a beachcomber. Beachcombers collect stones for the beauty intrinsic to each, while geologists aim to understand how an entire beachful of stones may have a common origin.

Of course, we don't wonder about such connections all the time; we are partly beachcomers, too. But even in beachcombing we can be stopped in our tracks by a deep, inner appreciation of the fact that these stones, this beach, these waters have been nudging each other back and forth in a kind of dance choreographed by fixed laws of nature — laws that hold for every beach in the world. The dance is universal, and we do well to admire it wherever it shows up, not so much to *understand* its patterns as simply to stand in awe.

Beach stones are just an example. In wondering about any number of things, our wonder converges upon the universe of things. Call it "reality" or "things as they are." It is one whole. It was there before we came and it will be there after we are gone. Have you ever had the sensation that all of nature is conspiring to communicate something to you, or at least is linked together in a single, massive purpose? If so, then you know what I'm referring to when I speak of the unity of nature as one interconnected "it" which elicits endless wonder.

You might think that I'm going to say that this "it" I've been referring to is really God. I don't believe that's true. In order to experience the difference between "it" — the awesome unity of all reality — and God, try the following heart-experiment. It has two parts.

First, look at some very ordinary object nearby — say, a tree or a pencil — and say "it" to yourself. Repeat "it" several times, trying to let your own wonder and awe rise to the surface. (This will not work if you have too many concerns on your mind; if that's the case, then wait until a time when practicalities have gone to sleep.)

Let that object be one instance of the "it" common to all real things; let your eyes roam around and see the same "it" in everything. This can also be done through hearing. Listen to just one sound in the orchestration of sounds that surrounds you. Say "it" about whatever is doing the humming, or banging, or chirping, and then let all the sounds you can hear represent the same "it" underneath all things, even the silent things.

Become aware of the fact that reality is what it is. Though we understand some of it, and are ignorant about much of it, "it" follows its own laws for existing.

Second, after you have some intuition of reality's stubborn independence, say the word "You." Don't you experience a change in the ascent of awe? A shift of gears? Don't you feel like a person lost in thought who suddenly realizes there is somebody else in the room?

Contemplating an "it" and contemplating a "You" are two different, though connected, experiences. In contemplating a "You," we experience feelings quite unlike the awe which "it" elicits.

We may feel either intrusion or joy at such a "You," but if by "You" we mean someone responsible for "it," then the connectedness of everything suddenly becomes overwhelmingly personal.

Please don't get the idea that I'm trying to prove the existence of God by this little heart-experiment. I take it for granted that you believe. However, I am trying to "define" God in a way that locates him and yet does not restrict him. To define God as, say, "the supreme being" doesn't do much for one's mind or heart. But to perform the above experiment does locate within our own experience the God who in fact means something to us.

LET us try the experiment again. That tree or that pencil is there. We know that the very fact that it exists has a lot to do with chance. That tree might not have ever been, had one seed not fallen in fertile ground years ago. But there it is now, obedient to the world's probabilities. The tree can be chopped down and cut into pencils, and the pencils sharpened into shavings, and the shavings burnt to smoke and ashes. Things acquiesce both in their emergence and in their demise.

As the tree stands there, doing exactly what is its nature to do, we can marvel at the order of nature in general, especially at how nature brings forth in any given acre of land living accommodations for the cohabitation of trees and grass, wind and birds and bugs. If we've studied any chemistry or biology we can marvel at the readiness of electronic valences to combine, given the chance, or at the steadiness of nitrogen cycles against chance. The burgeoning world is enmeshed in probabilities that boggle the mind.

But let us say "You" again. "You" know those probabilities. What we might feature as mindless chance is in reality the product of "Your" mind. "You" know that a chance meeting with an old friend on the street belongs to the ultimate sense of the universe.

Notice how even though wonder seems to bog down in too many unanswered questions whenever it ventures into the field of chance, we acknowledge some sense in it all by saying "You" to the one who created that field. We don't necessarily know what that sense is. Scientists unravel few of these things and do so rather slowly. But we are assured that things do make some sense whenever we let their cause be an intelligent and caring "You." Even when we don't explicitly utter "You," curious wondering seems meant to turn into awestruck wondering when our questions bring us to the brink of the unknown.

We live in a universe of probabilities for a very good reason. It allows each person to have a unique biography, a life unfixed by deterministic laws — and that, in turn, makes each person's being in love with God an absolutely and eternally unrepeatable reality. We know this when we bring any day — whether lucky or unlucky — to God in prayer at night. If nothing in our day merely "happens" but is under God's providential guidance through probabilities, then each day is a special gift. It is through the realization of probabilities that all of our biographies join together to make up the history of God's love for all men and women. To lie down at night saying "nothing merely happened" is the beginning of the prayer of praise — a prayer that ends by saying, "Your Kingdom came, today."

So far, we have wondered about insects, pencils, noises and trees, letting our curiosity turn to awe and letting awe turn to friendliness towards the "You" behind it all. But there comes a point in the lives of reflective adults when one begins to wonder about wonder itself. This real world that we contemplate is a whole, of which we contemplators are a part. We are not uninvolved observers of reality. The universe of real things includes us appreciating it. Reality has sprouted the means to reflect upon itself, question itself, and come to like itself. This wonder about wonder itself is the beginning of philosophy.

While you or I, sitting contemplatively in a park, pay respect to a tree's rustling obedience to wind and rain, while we marvel at the way the tree plays unreluctant host to chattering birds and squirrels, another person in the park may be marvelling at *us.* Of all the wonderful things on that person's horizon, there is something further to be astonished about: only human beings can wonder. The obedience of human beings to their possibilities is not, like trees and birds, a passive submission. It is an active creation, an evolution from within, full of deliberate intention.

What is wonder for? Why has the universe set conditions for a biosphere in which certain animals enjoy the capacity to raise a question? But not just one question: raise any question, discover some answers, and spend a lifetime searching, no matter how many answers have been found. Why does a woman or a man sitting on a park bench silently pore over ineffable questions?

Again, we can turn to where we know the answers lie: "You."

We begin to see what "You" are up to, why "You" have planted in us a ravenous, gnawing wonder that never says "enough." Augustine saw it: You have made us for yourself, and our hearts are restless until they rest in You. We did not wander into your house by accident. You have driven us in by your Spirit. When we were young, we saw here the evidence of your intelligence and wisdom. Now we see the evidence of your fierce passion. You want us with you. You will let nothing else satisfy us. You insist that we come intelligently and responsibly, that we suffer a lifetime of unanswered questions and halting convictions rather than suppress the wonder in our hearts that seeks your face.

I have been speaking here of a world-vision — one that sees the universe as "groaning in one great act of giving birth" and sees human wonder as the Spirit's first fruits. This vision has some very practical consequences for prayer. When we wake up in the morning and roll out of bed, it is not pure habit that gets us on our feet. Even when we sleep in on a Saturday, we eventually are driven out of bed by things that concern us — eating breakfast, reading the paper, meeting a friend, cleaning the kitchen. We "get up" because we are "up to" something. In other words, it is *purpose* that wakes us up and sets our minds and bodies in motion. It is not simply the things we are concerned about that wake us up. Our concern itself is the driving force.

This inner-born concern is not entirely our own possession, even though nature tends to make it habitual in us. We are carried along by inner impulses which, virtually by their own power, turn our heads to pay attention to our world in its unfinishedness.

Again, the simplest morning prayer is "You." We are up because "You" have already been up — up to planting in our hearts the Spirit that seeks your face. So we don't need so much to *intend* to seek God as to acknowledge that the Spirit of God is the driving force that nudged us out of bed.

It is very important here not to slip into a moralism about prayer. Prayer is not altogether a "should" in our lives. The only "should" we are under is that we should let what is implicit become explicit. We should cooperate with the dynamism of our restless wonder by naming not only its endpoint, but also its starting-point: "You."

HUMAN wonder about human things has another baffling twist to it that wonder about non-human things doesn't have. If I look at a maple tree and think it's an elm, I'm simply wrong. The maple tree stays a maple tree. But if I look at a friend and think that the friendship is becoming somewhat estranged, my thoughts partly create the reality I think I'm perceiving. The friendship does become somewhat estranged if only by virtue of my thinking so.

The reason for this peculiar phenomenon is that a friendship is partly constituted by human interpretations. Any change in thought about it is a change in the thing itself. The same is true, as we will see, of our successes and failures, our commitments and cares. Let us explore this path of wonder now; we will find again that the Lord is in it from beginning to end.

A teacher I once had, who died recently, spent fifteen years of his life writing a book on science, only to discover a mistake in viewpoint serious enough to make him junk the whole work.

Was he a failure or a success? He certainly "failed" to achieve what he had set out to do. And yet he did "succeed" in discovering a blind alley; and in science, the great majority of experimenters do nothing more than warn their colleagues which way *not* to go. But whether he was a success or a failure depends a lot on what he thought he was.

As it happened, he did earn a great deal of respect for his intellectual honesty. But despite others' opinions, he certainly must have wondered about himself. In particular, he must have wondered what the words "success" and "failure" really mean.

I imagine that he had the problem that we all have. If we don't know the meanings of the words we use to assess ourselves, aren't we in serious danger of calling our successes failures and our failures successes? This is what I mean by the baffling twist in the ascent of wonder when we wonder about our own selves.

Like the ascent of wonder about the non-human world, our wonder reaches a point of awe, except that now that awe is laced with a hefty shot of terror. The value of our friendships, of our commitments, of our very selves is now at stake. We don't mind being wrong about trees, but to be wrong about our own lives would be the worst possible mistake.

We must not think that only the proud talk about success. We all measure day-to-day "success" as well as "failure." We have to if we are trying to improve things. But we generally do that measuring by comparing our activities against pre-set goals. The terror of living is glimpsed when we wonder whether those goals themselves are worth stamping our one-and-only lives with. Is it a mistake to take this job? Should I marry this person? Is it wise to have another child?

The most intelligent persons in the world have no less difficulty in answering such questions. And this gives us a clue about what sort of answers we are after. We are not looking for intellectual certitude. Rather, we are looking for moral goodness and personal company. We trust, for example, the advice of people we call "good." This goodness is not intelligence; though it is not stupidity either. The good people whose moral judgments we trust tend to be kind, wise, and rather long-suffering. More than that, they are people who, after we have sought their advice, usually stick with us through the decision as if their own lives were at stake, too. We find them company in the heart, wanting what we want.

Now these good people are themselves not beyond criticism. But in what we look for *from* them we can see what we look for *beyond* them — from the "You" towards whom their own wonder as well as ours heads. When we bring the turning-point decisions of our lives to our "You," we look for both his own moral goodness and his personal company. That is, not only do we want guidance for our consciences, we also want our choice to be what God longs to do himself. And because he is God, he can be that heart-company in a manner no mere human friend ever could. Where friends can join us in desire, God can also be the source of our desire.

Moral success and failure, then, naturally depend on something profoundly interpersonal. We want our friends and mentors to share our purposes, but the heart's sweetest possibility is to be given a share in the purposes of the "You" beyond all criticism.

In the case of my teacher with the book in his wastebasket, he is a "success" if, after plowing through the necessarily painful thicket of bad feelings, he was able to say "I know I wanted to try it, my God, and I believe you gave me that desire. Had you pointed in any other direction, I would have left everything and followed."

WONDER does more than probe the ultimate meanings of "success" and "failure." Wonder rises because it also wants to understand what's really going on in very particular circumstances.

A father wonders what has happened to the little girl inside his teenage daughter. An aging employee wonders why he let himself be retired at sixty, albeit with gold watch and office party. A woman asks her brother what he meant when he said, "You never put any expectations on me." And then there are the desperate times when two persons are at each other's throats, each accusing the other of stances that were never taken. Every subsequent explanation is about as effective as trying to disentangle a snarl of coat-hangers with one more hanger.

It is a mark of genuine interior fidelity if we do not easily let our wonder rest with cogent explanations about these painful wonderments just because they make some sense. A cogent explanation is not necessarily a correct one. And in spite of the fact that our wonder is a trustworthy question-raiser, we ought not feel obliged to feed it simple answers just to keep it quiet.

Oh, but if wonder has no certainties, how relentlessly it churns until some homogeneous explanation starts to form! The mind labors over questions such as these:

> *Am I being rejected or accepted?*
> *Are we all pulling together on this or not?*
> *What makes that lady tick?*

But satisfying answers seldom come to stay. There do appear, however, beguilingly simplistic answers which, like the mythological basilisk, hypnotize us if we stare at them for long and blind us to the more complex explanations.

Still, to go without understanding, and to let our thirst for clarity go unslaked, is a physically and perhaps even a chemically painful ordeal. I suspect that the reason why we drink too much, or try to squeeze more out of sex than is there, is often to ease the blank pain of being ignorant about the particulars that really concern us.

That pain is a teacher of wisdom. Ask any old person whose eyes still twinkle. They have suffered long-forgotten questions about what was really going on and have watched these questions gradually merge into one question — and with one answer:

> *Do we really need to* ***understand*** *how it all hangs together? No. We need only to* ***trust*** *that it does hang together.*

Rising wonder, while it wants to understand, still needs, as its guiding star, a kind of trust. The very expectation that no reality is ultimately absurd assures even cool-headed scientists that within their fields no "gap" exists in which things make no sense at all. Most of humanity trusts the ultimate coherence of things, but how few of us, in the teeth of our own confusion, ever step back and bring that trust to mind. And fewer yet do so in an interpersonal way, turning to the trustworthy ground of everything with the word "You" on our lips.

To turn to our "You" is so simple and yet so liberating. Merely stepping away from our situation gives a moral distance from which to look at things in perspective. But more than that, when we enter the company of the one who made us subject to this ignorance in the first place, we experience one very practical liberation. I'm talking about the personal freedom to consider how much we ourselves are part of the problem. "Perhaps the problem is *me,* not the situation." If every person involved in a difficult affair turned to our common "You" with this kind of objectivity in mind, the situation would unravel a lot more quickly.

It may not be easy to assess our own roles in sticky

human affairs. Like changing our clothes, we are embarrassed to change our minds in public. We need a private time and place to divest ourselves of old views and to consider seriously whether a new view will wear better. In that seclusion, however, we are not really alone. There is one who knows, one who sees, one who loves to share with us his own liberating objectivity.

NOT all situations remain uncomprehended. That same trust which expects an underlying order in things also expects that at least some hidden disorders can be uncovered and abolished — particularly the inaccuracies and anomalies that hide within the very words we use to describe our relations to one another. Think of words like "cop-out," "jealousy," "familial," "democratic," "bossy," and so on. Although such words have common currency, isn't it our almost universal experience that nobody likes being labeled with them? All people consider themselves to be special cases. We don't like being classified under some category, not even flattering ones. It's not because we consider categories useless — we still use them for others — but because the categories seldom explain what inner struggles we went through to get to where we are.

Notice the difference. "Jealousy," "familial," and so on, describe outward behavior; they do not explain inner causes or historical developments. The meanings we humans are after when we try to understand our relationships may start off being descriptive, but they fail to satisfy our wonder until we can explain what has happened to this or that specific group of people.

Ultimately it's not the meanings of the words we're after anyway; it's the meaning of a situation involving people we care for. We want our words to work for us, but without prejudice to the delicacy and nuances that make each human interaction an absolutely special case.

How, then, can we guide the ascent of our wonder about human relationships? Obviously, we have to let those arrangements be what they are and not stuff them into word-boxes that fail to explain all the data. We should look with eyes full of open questions and be ready to have to grope for words to express what we see.

Fortunately, wonder can turn and reflect on its own progress. That is, we have the marvelous capacity to be bothered by further questions. We may settle on an explanation for a while and choose specific words to express it because the explanation answers most questions. But as long as further questions are allowed, wonder can criticize its own performance and build up a store of wisdom against the heart's usurping certitudes, bright ideas, and noisy claims.

Wonder, the quiet and relentless source of honest questions, has earned a reputation among the wise for getting at reality as it really is. Wonder knows, for example, that human relationships are dramas, and that those dramas have as their principals the wondering interiors of other men and women. It expects the plot to be about wonder getting sidetracked by people not knowing the difference between better and worse and not knowing how to turn within to one's own intellectual conscience for guidance. It has learned in the school of experience the path and the pitfalls of wonder. And it is keen to discern the difference between wonder's path and wonder's pitfalls in everyday life.

When it comes to probing human relationships, wonder enjoys the privilege of joining in the creative act of the "You" it worships. Just as God's Spirit brooded over the raging ocean and uncoupled light and darkness, so the Spirit of Wonder broods over human chaos to discern the light of meaning from the darkness of absurdity. That "You" has generated the wonder in us which, in spite of the fact that our upbringing and culture shape its purview, can turn *upon* the very history that conditions it and can make some sense out of it. In other words, history may condition us, but history is meaningless without the questions that occur to us through God's Spirit. History begs its Lord to illumine it through our wonder. And the Lord chose not to illumine it in any other way.

SOMETIMES we wonder what is going on and leave it at that. These are the times when our wonder likes to lie back and appreciate what it has come to understand. More often, however, whether we find out what's going on or not in a particular situation, we are forced to consider what action to take. Usually the reason we wondered what was going on in the first place was that we had to size up a situation that called for action.

Wondering what to do has a pain much like the pain of wondering what is going on — the pain of refusing facile options, the pain of having to act because time has run out, the pain of knowing that often the responsible thing to do involves inflicting pain on others. But the pain of facing action is a lot more piercing and is a great deal more capable of choking off wonder's high aspirations than is the pain of facing ignorance.

The reason is that in wondering what's going on we pose as spectators of a drama, while in wondering what to do we are involved as participants. The participants in a drama, unlike the spectators, are themselves transformed by the choices they make as one scene succeeds another. A decent person is produced by decent choices, just as a hero emerges from heroic choices on stage. The issue is not only what to make of the situation, but, more crucially, what to make of oneself. The risk of tragic decisions and a tragic outcome to one's life is an ever-present menace. It is no wonder that so many of us fail to act at all. Even though that failure too produces a "failure" who is a person, we seem to prefer to slip off quietly into the wings rather than risk becoming a tragic failure on the public stage.

Authentic action lies somewhere between timidity and cocksureness. We may have been able to say, "I know *the* truth about what's going on," but we never say, "I did *the* best about what needed doing." Instead, we report, "I did *my* best about what needed doing." We are forced to leave the judgment of what *the* best might have been to some indefinite future. In the meantime, situations unfold no matter what we do. Even when indecision paralyzes us, outcomes have our names on them. Those who trust that a discerning wonder will ferret out its prey overcome their timidity without ending up cocksure.

We all know people who manage to act with moral conviction but seldom turn to God. It's a pity. There is nothing like having company in doing good — especially when we feel tentative about the value of our efforts. Imagine how reassuring would be the company of the wisest and kindest person we know, somebody who was there not to tell us what to do, but rather to let us simply see the reaction on his or her face when we plunge into action. That Somebody is there.

Those who are in love with that Somebody — and know they are so in love (for many love unknowingly) — trust not merely their own capacity to wonder. They trust Somebody, a "You" to whom they can be grateful for giving them that benevolent wonder in the first place. This is company like no woman or man on the face of the earth can ever give. Even though many spiritualities regard God basically as a "friend," it would be a serious mistake, I believe, to make friendship the central model of his uncanny love. Our friends may wonder along with us, or be the object of our wonder, but they do not give us our wondering itself.

Those who turn to this wonder-giver as "You" enjoy something beyond even the joy of sharing in the creative act that distinguishes the light of meaning from the darkness of nonsense. They enjoy the honor of bringing about the betterment of the world hand-in-hand with the "You" who creates it. Their collaborative wonder not only operates *upon* history, through understanding it; it operates *behind* history, turning history off the paths of self-destruction through a communal discernment and action. Can you believe it? They not only think with God, they act with God. God redeems the world through their penchant for getting into the thick of it and straightening things out.

IN the foregoing heart-experiments we have been speaking of the ascent of wonder and reflecting on how natural it is to turn to the "You" we love when wonder seems to reach a plateau. This is prayer. It has a natural place in the quest of our spirits for the true and the good and the beautiful. What that place is, however, is not always clear. I would like to leave our heart-experiments now and turn to reflect in more depth on why we so easily fall out of real prayer. If prayer is so natural to our spirits, why does it so often feel like a dead-end?

One reason why many people lose the habit of

prayer is that they pray in an unnatural way and find it unsatisfactory. It is unnatural, for example, to come to prayer with an emotional problem and expect that the "power of prayer" will work like psychological therapy. Prayer can and does mediate healing, but hardly in the way that psychologists do. A woman I know — let us call her Lucy — struggled with this tension between psychology and prayer and worked through it extraordinarily well, I believe. Her struggle is typical of the struggle we all have with assessing our own value as human beings, but it also reveals just where prayer's power really lies.

Lucy is fifty-five years old and single. For a number of years she has suffered from a lack of self-confidence. Being very intelligent, she has been able to understand how her problem stemmed from the way she was raised, and she has been able to meet her responsibilities very well in spite of what she has suffered personally.

Recently — a Pentecost Sunday, as a matter of fact — the breakthrough came. I can't explain how, nor do I think I need to describe the events that led up to the breakthrough. It is not a logical development; it is a leap of sorts. But she did have some things to say about self-confidence that describe how wonder paradoxically does not have to know what it is asking for — does not even have to know it is asking.

"I really didn't know what self-confidence was although I surely knew what it was like to be without it," she said. "I'm now in touch with myself. I know what 'secure' means, and I can depend on what I feel inside and believe, instead of always going by what other people think."

She talked about how for years she had wearied herself with analyzing, hitting all the symptoms but never striking the root. "It came with a 'bang.' I still have problems, but I'm at one with myself now. I'm satisfied to stay in the present, and I'm not always anxious about the future and the past. I feel as though I have finally fallen into my nitch. I can handle my problems with confidence."

I asked her whether this was the moment when she really found God. Surprisingly, she said No. "I have been at one with God in my deepest being," she said, "but not in my 'psychology.' Then that part of me, too, joined the deeper part of me where I am at one with God."

Lucy had been faithful to prayer throughout all this, but she avoided what we might call "false prayer." She did not try to disconnect herself from her dilemma during prayer, as though she were supposed to be praying over Scripture or praying for the needs of others and not having these "selfish" thoughts. She brought herself before the Lord just as she was. And even there, she did not pretend to know whether she was asking God to give her the grace of inward confidence or whether she was simply offering herself for God's own kind purposes.

She was like a man I heard about a long time ago who hobbled to church every day on a bad leg. When asked what he does when he prays, he answered that all he said was: "God, . . . Leg!"

There is a time to ask for specific healings; there is a time to offer our sufferings to the Lord; and there is a time just to hobble into his company and trust.

This doesn't mean that all genuine prayer simply waits to see whether or not God will give us what we think we need. God does give us all we really need. We must believe that. True prayer lets God, who knows our needs, give us what we don't easily recognize.

For this reason we can say that we don't need patience as much as trust. Patience can look very much like trust, but it easily presumes that God is holding back somehow, forcing us to "wait" for some divine visitation in the future. Trust, however, while it may wait for consolation, still believes that God never holds himself back in the darker hours. The anguish of confusion and frustration *are* the groans of God's own Spirit bringing each person's small embryo of space and time to birth.

ANOTHER reason why people lose the habit of prayer is that, for all its apparent simplicity, it is no small thing to turn to our "You." To utter our "You" in any genuine way presumes that a profound conversion has taken place in our hearts. Conversion to God happens only when we have already been disillusioned by the world, with its easy words of certitude. It means treating our own ideas and certitudes with a ready skepticism; it means becoming a person on a quest for life's genuine measures; it means getting up in the morning and meeting with one's business as though life were a courageous risk.

For many people it means a complete turn-around regarding what we know and what we don't.

The turn-around may begin like this: We spend a good number of years thinking that we know a lot about life and that we know very little about God. Then, as we wonder about what the measure of genuine self-confidence, courage, patience, freedom, and so on really are, we realize that our ideas about ourselves are just hypotheses — trial-and-error experiments, so to speak — and that we are our own guinea pigs.

The trial we can stand, but the error, in our own case, is lethal. For we realize the permanent and deadly possibility that we can be self-deceived about our own virtues and shortcomings for an entire lifetime.

In every real case of such a turn, we pivot on a concrete problem of our own — not on any abstract reflection that humanity in general lacks the means to guide itself, nor on any concrete examples from the lives of others, such as I am offering here. Some, for example, find themselves desperately alone, but quite uncertain that "alone" is the proper word for their pain. Some feel crushed by guilt-feelings, but quite uncertain what portion of these feelings represents true guilt. Some seem to spend a lifetime trying to please others, but quite uncertain how pleasing they are in themselves. But you and I each have our own pivot-points. Friends may help us recognize them, but the turn we make in solitude with God.

We turn in awe and in trust to a "higher power," to a "You." We bring our dilemma before him — "God, . . . Leg!" We become transformed into reverse agnostics — very suspicious about the certainties people derive from their own experiences and very confident about what we discern in prayer. Obviously, it takes time to learn from prayer; it takes a certain "taste" for God's way. And we can get that taste from the examples of other people of prayer in our history and among our friends, if we are so blessed. But the turning point comes when we realize that we know practically nothing about life but possess one very precious truth about God.

When I say we know one very precious truth about God, I don't necessarily mean that we have the sort of knowledge that is borne primarily by concepts or an ethics. Such knowledge about God comes, but only as the result of a more basic, more personal sort of knowledge. The precious truth is simply this:

God is trustworthy.

I want to call this kind of knowledge "Assurance." It is not like getting an insight into what is going on in a particular situation. Assurance is something we need to survive the ordeal of *not* knowing what's going on. Nor is it like having moral conviction about how to behave in this or that situation. There, too, Assurance is needed in order to act in spite of moral confusion.

Assurance is knowing a truth: that God is trustworthy. Knowing that God is trustworthy, though, does not come the same way as knowing, say, that terriers are jumpy. We know terriers are jumpy because we have been accosted by the plain evidence. The evidence that God is trustworthy is not so plain. We believe it to be true only because we have already let ourselves trust God. It is a knowledge based more on acting than on reasoning.

This is not an unusual sort of knowledge. As infants, most of us have had great doses of Assurance from our mothers and fathers. Even those who, sad to say, were deprived of it, know at least that something was missing. We grew up assured that reality was roughly stable and enduring, that there were answers to at least some questions, that life is worth effort and sacrifice. We believed these things to be true because we believed *in* our parents. And when it comes to believing *in* someone, one doesn't run a credit check.

There is a magnificent harmony between the Assurance good parents give and the Assurance God gives. When a mother comforts her distressed child, she says, "There, there, now. Everything will be all right." Does she say it just to put the child at ease? No, she also believes that everything *will* be all right. Whether or not she speaks of God, she trusts that human wonder will not be ultimately frustrated.

Still, children must grow up and claim that Assurance for themselves. As adults, you and I may continue to feel support just by watching how other adults let God assure them in difficult times. But being an adult also means carrying a load of responsibilities of our very own — burdens with nobody else's name on them but ours, with each one of us bearing an unwritten biography whose chapters contain unheard-of turns of fortune and unhearalded feats of heroism.

All the intelligence and wisdom and dedication we have been able to muster would have been inaccessible to us had we not let ourselves be assured by the evidence of our own wonder. Indeed, even the certitudes we have reached about the world of each one's experience — for example, that one is made to love, or that life's enemies are found within human hearts — were reached only because we trusted that the welling up of wonder within has the power to test every truth and falsehood along the way. No human being who has ever made sense out of his or her experience, no human being who has ever done something truly worthwhile in the world, has ever done so without having first trusted "something assuring."

I put quotation marks around "something assuring" for two reasons. First, not everybody who turns to God names where they turn "God." In fact, not everybody even thinks about what they do when they take the risks of doing good at a high cost to themselves. I believe such people deserve our profound respect; they deserve the support we can give by acknowledging with them that we humans have to act with at least some sort of Assurance beyond us if we are to live intelligently and wisely. In other words, we will give them far more support by *not* talking about "God" (and all the dull associations the word can connote), but by talking about the marvel of human wonder and the Assurance it depends on.

Secondly, those who do name where they turn for

Assurance "God" can sometimes be turning in fact away from their own burden, their own selves, and their own destiny in God. This happens when they forget what "God" really means to them. Think, for example, of a priest who is faithful to celebrating Mass every day. How many times has he mouthed "Lord God, Heavenly King, Almighty God and Father" and thought of himself as merely leading a congregation of equally mindless voices? It is embarrassingly easy to replace our own unique experiences of trusting God in harried times with a blander set of concepts — familiar to all, but emptied of the power of first-hand experience to inspire awe.

This is the graver danger, and this is a constant danger.

This is the same danger as not knowing the real meanings of the words we use to measure ourselves, except that here we don't know the meaning of the one word that can make sense of all words. "God" can become just a noise in the mouth.

A few years ago I heard a rather humorous parable that supposedly illustrated what "trusting God" really means — though I believe it better illustrates how banal our notions of God have become. It goes like this:

> A man was out walking in a dense fog near a cliff overlooking a deep chasm.
>
> Unfortunately, he stepped off the cliff.
>
> Fortunately, a branch was there, which he grabbed.
>
> Unfortunately the branch started cracking.
>
> Fortunately, he believed in God and cried out for help.

> Unfortunately, God merely said, "Do you trust me?"
>
> Fortunately, the man said, "Yes!"
>
> Unfortunately, God said, "Then let go of the branch."
>
> Fortunately, he did let go, and he fell only three inches onto a broad, safe ledge.
>
> Moral: Trust God and he will help.

I feel obliged to add one final line:

> Unfortunately, the real God is not like this at all.

Did not the real God let six million of his Chosen People be incinerated a generation ago? And did not the real God let the one person who most embodied him be abandoned, insulted, tortured, and finally murdered on a cross?

The word "God," then, refers to someone or something terrifying. The God-of-the-broad-safe-ledge is a picture we paint on a large billboard as if to block our vision of God as he really is and distract us from the inner terror over life as we get it.

We who easily use the word "God" have to be extremely careful not to let the word refer to a safe, predictable, speechless idol of our own making. The Old Testament term "Yahweh" stands for a pronunciation of God's name, which was lost because the Jews forbade themselves even to utter it — evidence of some bit of caution lest they begin to fashion God in their own image.

Like them, we have to make sure that the term "God" always derives its meaning from our own concrete experiences of wonder and awe, of helplessness and fear, of desire and hope, and of the ways God has become incarnate in our history.

3

GOD'S WORD

WHO might this "You" be that is so terrifying and yet so Assuring? If he were to speak one clear word to us directly, would we be pulverized where we stand or would we stand all the more firm?

When we turn to the "You" in trust, do we even get any response? Is our trust merely a blind waiting for life to get over with? Or do we receive any guidance that will help us live responsibly and intelligently?

Our faith teaches us that this Word of Assurance comes to us in the person, the life, of Jesus of Nazareth. That is, for each of the different ways in which our wonder can approach the "You" it seeks, that "You" speaks a saving word that can be found incarnated in the encounter of Jesus with those he loved.

Let me rephrase that; I cannot overemphasize how important it is: Absolutely every kind of question that we can raise about the significance of what we think or say or do has its answer in the Good News of Christ Jesus. I'm simply putting in contemporary terms the ancient belief of the Christian community that salvation in Christ Jesus is sufficient.

No doubt, professed Christians will state their

belief that Jesus is God's own Son, sent for our salvation. Many may feel ready to die for that belief. But do we understand what it means? Do we automatically regard the Word of Assurance in Jesus as an intelligible, direct response to all our inner questions of wonder? In short, is everything our heart seeks really being met when we embrace the Gospel?

We grow rather used to the biblical expressions "saved," "forgiveness of sins," "reconciled," without knowing exactly which experiences of our own they refer to. The tendency is to form narrowly religious interpretations of them that have little to do with our so-called "secular" activities.

The very earliest texts in the New Testament proclaimed merely that Jesus *is* Lord. After that, all the epistles and Gospels filled out, in prayers, instructions, story and myth, the meaning of that proclamation for Jews or Gentiles of the period. The expressions "saved," "reconciled," and so on, already meant something to the people who heard the disciples' preaching. They referred to an acknowledged need for what we have gingerly called "something assuring." The basic proclamation was that, no matter how that need is spoken of, it is fulfilled in Jesus of Nazareth, God's Anointed. In him everything that hearts have been yearning for will be found.

In the past few decades, biblical theologians have made great strides in understanding the thought-forms of New Testament times. Their work is necessary if we are going to understand Scripture. But being a Christian requires something a great deal more than knowledge. It requires that each of us welcomes the Assurance that comes through Jesus. The meaning and scope of that Assurance come mainly from reading the text of our hearts before reading the text of Scripture: What is it that my heart cries out for? Whither does wonder head? What do I need in order not to violate other persons — or even my self? What would make me a genuinely "free" human being?

Notice that we put the question in terms derived from existential thought: "heart," "wonder," "person," "free." New Testament Jews framed the question in terms of Old Testament promises, and Paul, when preaching to Greeks, had to speak of their "unknown God." There will always be different frameworks employed to express the question, but all people experience an as-yet-unfulfilled orientation to "something assuring."

We Christians have experienced in the Jesus of our history an Assurance that meets our question. But we cannot understand what the biblical words "salvation" and so on refer to unless we each experience that Assurance where we cry out for it. In short, we need to connect the words of the Gospel with something concrete in our own experience.

Let us try the following exercise. We speak of the Gospel itself as "Good News." What *is* this news that is so good? Can we put it in a sentence? Can *you* put it in a sentence?

Try.

In a moment, I will put it into a sentence as I see it, but my words are not your words. Our words for the

Word will differ, one person to another. My formulation stands for my struggle for life, just as your formulation stands for yours. I don't mean to suggest that mine will be better. I mean only to illustrate the principle that the "Good News" must be experienced as *personally* good and as relevant to the entire range of each person's actual life.

What is it, then, about Jesus of Nazareth that consoles you most? It has to be more than the mere fact that in this world of unbelief you have a belief to cling to. What is it about that belief that is so Assuring to you?

Nor is it enough to say "I am saved from my sins." You still sin, do you not? If you still think of yourself as "saved," what are you saved *from?* And what are you saved *for?*

Suppose you were to preach the "Good News" to, first, a teenager, then a lawyer, and then an elderly pensioner. Is there some kernel of news in your own experience of life that each of them can recognize and welcome?

For my part, I see Jesus as "Assuring" because he himself was someone Assured. That is, through the many turns in his life, he trusted the "You" upon which all wonder converges. Jesus lived the poverty of having to turn outside of his own ego for reliance. When it came to the crises of opposition, misunderstanding, and even death, he did not compromise. Worried and fearful though he clearly was, he went forward with the Assurance that there was no *need* to worry or fear.

And something happened to Jesus, something beyond his death, something that convinced those who believed in him that death *need not* be destructive of human life. Because he acted as one Assured, and because that Assurance was justified in that uncanny event we call the "resurrection," Jesus himself becomes God's Assurance to us that we are never abandoned.

The "Good News," as I would put it, is found very concisely in Philippians 4: 5-6:

> *The Lord is very near; there is no need to worry.*

Christian or not, people of all ages worry and fear. It's part of our nature's early-warning system to protect both ourselves and those we care for. It is quite legitimate. But there is a deeper level of worry that can paralyze us and prevent us from taking the personal risks necessary to do some good in the world. It's not a worry about external threats. Rather it's a worry about internal resources.

For example, I worry whether I'm intelligent enough to ever understand current political affairs. I worry whether I'm realistic enough to face some hard truths about the future. I worry whether I'm benevolent enough to serve others in a way that really does them good.

More on the dark side, I worry that when life's pressures rise I will give in to compromises, inner lies and false absolutes — anything to ease the spiritual pain of watching my hopes turn impossible for me.

Ultimately, I worry whether the "You" my heart

seeks really welcomes me.

The "Good News" for me is that there is no need to worry at these deeper levels. This is paradoxical because I'm *not* assured that I *do* have the inner resources to solve life's riddles and meet life's challenges. I may well fall short or head down an altogether wrong path. What the life, death, and "resurrection" of Jesus reveal to me is that it is enough to obey within. That is, it is enough to *meet* life's problems in obedience to my inner wonder's quest and to utter my "You" at wonder's far pole.

Jesus was obedient within unto death. Death on a cross, yes, but long before that, he was obedient within unto all the deaths required by a life totally dependent on the "You" his heart sought. He wanted to prepare the Jewish people for the coming of a spiritual Kingdom — and he died to that. He wanted to heal and comfort — and he died to that too. He wanted at least a few disciples to understand and stand by him . . . still another death. Jesus watched his longing wonder's highest ideals escape his grasp, but he still obeyed that wonder's humble yielding: "Not my will but Yours be done."

He was crucified, laid in a tomb, and left for dead. Then something happened. He did not "come back to life" the way Lazarus did. None of the witnesses believed that. Something else happened, something that involved his physical body, but not something primarily about the body. The external reports differ: some may touch him, some may not; some see him, some do not; some of the seers believe, some do not;

some of the non-seers believe, too, and some do not. But all believers proclaim one central fact: God has done this so that we might find the life we are made for. He has fulfilled every Old Testament hope and promise as well as every hope and promise any human wonder ever entertains.

The event of the Resurrection is a *saving* event. We don't need to know "what actually happened" in the sense that television or newspaper reporters use the term. To know "what actually happened" in a *saving* way, we have to welcome Jesus' fearlessness of death and his absolute conviction of God's love as a present possibility for ourselves. The Resurrection is easy to understand, but if, and only if, we understand our own experience of being saved from our own wonder's deepest fears through believing that Jesus is the reply of the "You" whom our wonder addresses.

WE said earlier that the "You" our hearts seek renders Assurance to any of our wonder's quests. In other words, in the life, death, and Resurrection of Jesus Christ, God gives an Assurance which is applicable to the entire range of human predicaments. Without that belief, our Christianity runs through only certain levels of our lives and leaves other levels entirely unaffected. But we should look at several examples in order to understand just how God's Word in Jesus really speaks to the variety of ordinary wonderments we encounter.

We wonder, for example, what real virtues would be like — virtues of courage, serenity, compassion. We can easily recognize these qualities in the behavior of others, but we do not really know what these words mean for ourselves before we actually become courageous, serene, compassionate, or self-confident in our own situations.

At the heart of the predicament of ours crouches a truth we hesitate to face: we have no sure way of knowing by ourselves what "better" this or "better" that really means. People brought up in an unjust social order do not know what a "better" social order would be like. A neurotic doesn't recognize "better" mental health when he or she comes near it. Courtroom lawyers might win most of their cases, but they seldom enjoy much certitude about whether their services have been for the "betterment" of individuals and of society at large.

We need some hint, though, do we not? We need some pre-taste of what quality living really is if we are going to recognize what it is we seek.

A few weeks ago I was riding my bicycle down a busy street and a taxi-driver pulled close in behind and laid on his horn to get me out of his way. What would have been the more "courageous" thing to have done? Ride as fast as I could until I reached a place to pull over? Gesture back something equally belligerent? Ignore him altogether?

"Courage" — I don't honestly know what it means and yet I wish I had it.

The pre-taste of real courage that comes to my mind

is the word of Jesus to turn the other cheek, to walk the second mile.

Ouch!

I can think of plenty of reasons for being pushy with the pushy, and I know I'd feel humiliated to let myself be scared out of somebody's way. But besides my reasons and my feelings, there's a far more important issue: I want true courage. I will be at odds with my own self if I don't have it.

I must confess that I didn't act very "courageously" that day. (What I did is between God and me . . . and one befuddled taxi-driver.) There was a lesson there for me, though. I have not only a general need for the word of God to discern true courage: I was in dire need of it then and there, on the street, when my pride insisted on reacting without any interference from wisdom. My best self was battling against my worst self. I was crying out for help without realizing where my cry was directed.

The whole scene now reminds me of the time when Jesus was slapped in the face by a Temple guard. It's the first time Jesus is recorded as being struck. The first slap hurts far more than all the ones that follow because it is unexpected, and up to that point one's "courage" remains untested and undefined.

We have all been "hit in the face" in one way or another. We can feel the swelling of outrage and revenge. That swelling, evil though it threatens to be, becomes the material for real prayer when we contemplate Jesus in this scene and experience in him the counter-swelling of true courage. We get a taste, a memory, a feel for what winning interior battles is like. True courage, as revealed by God in Jesus and as tested by countless persons of integrity, is primarily the guts to face interior enemies rather than exterior ones. This I now know from the Gospel.

ENOUGH of individual virtues. What about social justice? Does our wonder find in Jesus some preview of what an entire social order might look like if social justice prevailed? He certainly didn't outline an ideal social structure. He seemed much more intent on naming the values that any community of people ought to hold, no matter under what form of social organization.

For instance: the absolute value of each person in the eyes not only of God but of every other person; or the special value of being childlike and poor because this external dependency is so close to the internal dependency of Jesus himself on God; or the radical turn-around in values that sees sin as the one fate that is literally worse than death.

Whether any country today can come to respect and embody these values in its social systems depends on the disvalues already operative there. This is obvious. But there is one over-riding Christian value that is easy to overlook. It is the value of an interior conversion of heart for the exterior social order.

It's easy to overlook because we tend to envision social justice as a set of external relationships of fairness among people, without paying equal attention to the internal acts that produce — even constitute — those relationships. Justice is not about external behavior. It's about the re-ordering of hearts wherein people are sincerely honored for their own sake. A so-called "unjust" social order may make it difficult for a just person to render that honor, but the injustice lies primarily in the cold hearts that don't give a damn for the neighbor. An entire social order may be called "unjust," but both its causes and its solutions operate in the hearts of real persons — individuals with names, addresses and phone numbers.

When Jesus accused the Pharisees of unjustly laying burdens on the poor, he said, "It's not what goes into persons that defiles them; it's what comes out of their hearts."

What does this mean for prayer? It means, first, that a prayer for social justice does get a response. God truly is Assurance where we need it. We can easily forget that when the odds against social reform seem insuperable. Then the world would begin to hold more sway over our hearts. We still might pray, but we would think of God as having only ears to hear; but no mouth to speak, no hands to act. His Assurance would dwindle down to a promise which no generation will see fulfilled. We would yearn for an afterlife even more intensely, because we hadn't heard any Assurance about this one.

Secondly, to hear God's response in Jesus we need to take to heart Jesus' own unswerving conviction that love of God and love of neighbor count more than anything else. God doesn't give us Assurance by equipping us with effective political strategies. Rather he responds by assuring us of the absolutely basic principle on which all truly "just" action must proceed: "You must love the Lord your God with all your heart, with all your soul, with all your mind, and with all your strength. And you must love your neighbor as yourself."

And finally, just as genuine prayer ought to spring from the soil of our own human experience, so the genuine Assurance we receive through Jesus ought to free our hearts and minds to eliminate injustice in that same soil. The Gospel can really free our hearts to face ridicule and confrontation without fear for our own egos. And the Gospel can really free our minds, too: it gives us the insight that the operative cause in what we call an "unjust social structure" is the unconverted heart. Whatever strategies we hammer out to better the situation, at least we won't compound the present injustice by trying to change merely the external behavior of oppressors for the sake of sheer external order for the oppressed.

So let us pray for social justice. But we are not lighting votive candles and walking away. God's Word thunders back: "Follow me! I am going to act through your actions!" There is no need to be timid; the Lord of life and death is very near.

Prayer is a dangerous occupation, is it not? The more we root it in wonder, the more God empowers *us* to act with his own integrity and fearless compassion. One of my favorite texts from the Old Testament is the line, "If you aspire to serve the Lord, prepare yourself for an ordeal!" (Sirach 2:1) Prayer is not like practicing tennis alone where we hit one ball after another over the net. It is more like the game itself: the balls get delivered back into our court.

IT'S becoming evident that wonder has two kinds of ends. There's what we might call the "horizontal" ends — the things in nature and history that concern us. And there's also the "vertical" end — the "You" that our hearts seek.

These two ends can be pursued simultaneously, even though one or the other may be more dominant in our consciousness. We can let go of our cares for a while and pray, knowing that prayer will give us strength to return to those cares. Or we may throw ourselves into those cares with the quiet trust that wonder has the power to bring us to our "You" again.

On the other hand, each of these ends can be pursued to the exclusion of the other. That's when we become unreal people, living in only half the real world. Those, for example, who feel too busy to pray or who call their work their "prayer" lose their taste for speaking *to* God. They speak *about* him, if they speak of him at all. I've met a number of people in retreats who, it turns out, spend their prayer *thinking* about God instead of talking or listening to him. They have grown afraid of prayer in the second person singular: "You."

Then there are those, fewer in number perhaps, who

shun involvements with practically all horizontal things because they want their path to God to be a straight, upward line. They have grown deaf to God's word in Jesus — the command that we love one another. This is the genuine, loving response on God's part to those who seek the truly straight path to him. We are to love one another not just because he commands it, but for a reason that is very easy to understand, though very demanding to carry out. In loving one another, we will find the fulness of God's self-gift. In other words, God's perfect revelation of himself includes one's neighbor — the lady next door whose face is a map of agony, or the nameless families of other cultures whose lives we touch whenever we pay money for anything. This "Good News" can be rather "Bad News" for those who suppress their cares for people around them.

THE "Good News" can also appear like "No News" to any of us suffering physical or emotional torments. For even though the Gospel can often make quite clear sense of our horizontal ends, there are also times when no such clarity seems to come.

This is the dark side of God's affair with us. Often we feel cursed by God — if we are physically crippled, for example, or neurotic, or find ourselves stuck with unmeetable responsibilities for spouse and children. Then wonder itself becomes an added suffering, with a pain quite unlike physical suffering. Where physical suffering cries out merely that it stop, this soul-suffering does not. The soul's agony is a passion for Someone, demanding an embrace, an Assurance.

This too is data on God as he really is. Not that God curses those he loves, but, as any Jeremiah will tell us, those he loves often feel condemned. We firmly believe that God knows all about our plight — but that only perplexes us more. And when we add the realization that God, through his Spirit, is also making us ask the very questions to which no answers seem to come, then we feel justified in railing against him. We utter our "You" in torment and frustration.

God does not explain why we, his loved ones, suffer. Theologians have tried to justify God's right to make such a world, but their arguments have never put an end to our wondering "why?" To be perfectly honest, we have to admit that we do not know.

Still, God has spoken his definitive word on human suffering. The word he has given is the "word" which is a person — his Son who suffers with us. Jesus is not a word of explanation, telling us "why." He is a word of assurance, telling us to trust. For he too trusted without knowing why his "You" had forsaken him. His cry, "Father, why have you forsaken me?" was not said for effect: he wanted to *know*. But he trusted anyway, and became God's Assuring word to all who carry a cross.

Is there any sense at all, then, which the crucified, trust-filled Jesus can give to human agony? Yes, there is. We may not understand why God lets us be tortured by human pain and ignorance, but our crucified forefather very clearly saw that human pain is not the worst evil that can befall us. The worst evil is sin. In a word, it is better to *suffer* evil than to *do* evil. Jesus may not have understood why the Father called him to agony, but he did understand that the only alternatives to that agony were the sins of pride and power towards which the Devil urged him.

What a horrible fate sin must be if human suffering can be thought of as a tolerable alternative! And how glorious must be those ordinary, unknown women, men, and children who endure untellable frustrations rather than give into their own pride!

We have every right to complain, when we turn to this "You" from the dark valley of suffering. The prophets did it, the Psalmists did it, Jesus did it. It may feel very much like hatred for God or at least searing resentment at our lot. Perhaps what scandalizes us most is the fact that the very darkness of spirit that we fled from in trying to be honest and good appears exactly like the darkness we encounter when we approach our awesome God.

But when we complain, we should not forget to ask "Is this the worst thing that could happen to me? This is the test, the bar of judgment before which all physical and existential pain must come. "Is this the worst thing?" If we take seriously the Good News — and the Awesome News — we must utter our "No." The worst thing is not to trust, to turn away deliberately from the "You" our hearts are made for. The worst thing may very well be to fail to respect the Lord enough to bother complaining.

HAVE you noticed that, even though we call the Gospel "Assurance" from God, our wonder itself is a form of Assurance, too? When we welcome the Gospel from the outside — whether in the life of Jesus or in the lives of Christians — we never questioned whether wondering itself might be a silly thing to do. We were counting on the fact that our wondering would not stop short of its goal. It may have been suppressed temporarily, but that beast of wondering went on devouring our consciousness.

We depended on wonder, we who are Assured. We trusted that something within us would become alarmed if we went astray, and would rejoice when we found the path again.

Besides Assurance from without, then, there is also Assurance from within. To put the same thing in more classical terms, besides the mission of the Son there is the mission of the Spirit. God Assures us with a Double Assurance, with one complementing the other. No one welcomes Jesus as Christ who is not already disposed by God's Spirit to seek him. Christ is called the light of the world; this is our faith. But without the "pilot light" of wonder already burning in human hearts, Christ can never set this world ablaze.

This doctrine of Double Assurance has an immediate and crucially important application to a certain kind of prayer — the prayer of discernment.

We all face decisions: large ones and small ones. Whether we turn to God or not, we all use some process of making a choice. We weigh pros and cons;

we feel our way through; we ask advice. No matter how we go about it, inner wonder is seeking to form an outer word.

Those who live in an interpersonal dialogue with God speak of decision-making as "seeking God's will" and as "discerning the spirits." These two expressions are quite accurate. Keep them in mind because recently a number of spiritual writers have jumbled them together and spoken of "discerning God's will" and thereby have lost sight of God's Double Assurance in discernment.

The expression "discern God's will" suggests the following simplistic picture: God has a will, a plan; it exists; and he wants us to do it. On our part, we are looking for what the plan might be; we don't yet know; but we have to look for it or beg God to tell us what it really is. Such a picture is heretical because it excludes the doctrine that we could not even begin to seek God were it not for his grace. In our terms, this doctrine is equivalent to saying that our spirit of wonder that seeks our "You" is God's own Spirit. We do "seek God's will," yes; God does have a specific will. But doing so requires that we "discern the spirits": that is, we weigh our inner impulses to discern which of them originate in God and which in our own autonomy.

The difference here is the difference between our aim and our method. We aim to carry out "God's will." But to accomplish that, we do not simply weigh the so-called "objective" worth of various proposals. Our method is to weigh the inner leaps and drives of wonder about such proposals and discern which of them seems most consonant with loving the heart's "You."

To this inner testing we add the outer Assurance of the Gospel. There we find divine values in flesh and blood. We are not after a slavish imitation of Jesus' behavior. The "Imitation of Christ" does not mean that. We are after the "feel" of a life that is truly salvific, a life that incarnates selfless love, freedom from material attachments, fearlessness of death, and a bottomless trust in God.

The decision, however, is still up to us. God does not choose for us in such a way that all we have to do is discover what he decided. Discernment means understanding the available options, testing the quality of wonder's ascent to them, and freely choosing between them. God's will enters the picture through the Double Assurance we need to make a choice that is really "free." Because God Assures us from within, we can be confident that we truly can make a choice out of love for him. And because God Assures us through the Gospel from without, we have a living example of God's own style of self-giving.

Does this leave God's Providence out of the picture? Yes it does, if by Providence we mean that God sees the future. Whether God sees the future or not has no bearing on the manner in which we "find his will." It also leaves out of the picture any notion of Providence which suggests that God governs human events by interfering in his own laws of nature and history — by "miracles," that is, which pre-arrange events for our sake. But if by Providence we mean that God has provided a love for him in our hearts and has provided an incarnation of him in our history, and that this is the absolute best he can provide for our sake, then a double Providence is what the picture is all about.

Having said all that about the method of "discerning the spirits," we still have to speak of our aim — "to seek God's will." All prayer of discernment has to begin by addressing God directly and asking him what it is that he wants. It's not exactly asking God to "reveal" his will, though, since we really will make a choice that is a free decision. Rather it is a statement of intention, inserting our individual purposes within the larger purposes of God. In short, it's asking God for the joy of shared purpose.

This notion of shared purpose is a rather recondite one, but accurate all the same. We do not "discover" God's will, as though it is already written down in some heavenly book. Nor, at the other extreme, do we decide autonomously what we think is best to do and just hope that God tolerates our incompetence. God "reveals" his will by the subtler gift of interior desire to do what pleases him, leaving us to choose freely what that might be. We truly share purposes with God at that point, just as truly as we share purposes with intimate friends. The big difference here is the miracle by which God gives us his own desire for very concrete actions in our world.

We had better take a concrete example of this because it is shamefully easy to talk about these things abstractly and not even consider that being Doubly Assured might require an inner conversion of our hearts. Let us imagine a "small" decision, too. It might better reveal how all-pervasive God's Double Assurance is in our lives.

Suppose one day you notice your neighbor hanging out laundry to dry. You ask him what happened to his dryer, and he says it broke down and the parts won't be delivered for several weeks. Something in you wants to let him use your own dryer and, simultaneously, something else in you says, "Don't." You can think of plenty of reasons not to make the offer: Your wife or husband ought to be consulted; right now you feel a genuine need for a more stable routine around the house; your own basement looks like the Goodwill Collection Depot; you don't feel up to establishing more ties with this particular neighbor, etc. On the other hand, the Gospel does say to love your neighbor; you don't want to get a reputation for being miserly; this might be an occasion to get to know this neighbor better, etc.

It's interesting, isn't it, that we can even throw the Gospel into the balance and not necessarily come up with a heartfelt decision. The reason is that in all good decisions we ought first to let wonder get in touch with its ultimate aim: "You; what do you want, my God?" Only then will the Gospel have any impact because the Gospel is then read not merely as a moral guideline applicable to many cases but as a personal response of Someone we address. I'm not saying that in this case the Christian choice is obvious; it is not.

But I am saying that to begin by turning to God and simply asking what he "wants," we experience a rather sudden freedom to "discern the spirits" that urge us in different directions at once.

We all know what it is to have strong wants. Think particularly of the wants that come out of our concern for those we love. When we turn to our Assurance and ask, "What do You want?" we are asking for a share in his own loving concern for our particular human situation. We are asking for the Assurance that by testing the inner forces that move us towards and against various options, and by freely making a choice out of love for God and being guided by the Gospel, we do in fact "do God's will." God's will is accomplished not because he told us his plan but because he has graciously taken up residence in our hearts himself and shares with us his own passionate desire for good in the world. Of this we can be Assured.

LITTLE by little, I've been trying to lead us gradually to a fully rounded view of the place of prayer in the human condition. Still, there is one incredible truth that I cannot ease my way into. It's too big a leap. So let me say it outright and then explain it by sketching the broad outlines of the structure of prayer in human history.

The truth is this: Jesus by himself is not the sum total of God's outer Assurance to the world; *we* are too.

So far we have been talking mainly about how the Spirit in our wonder goes about seeking the Word from God. But wonder does not always seek. When wonder receives strength from the Gospel or makes a decision under the impulse of God's Spirit to respond to the needs of others, then wonder welcomes God's word and rejoices in that embrace. Whenever you and I welcome the light of the Gospel and act on Gospel values, we are not *seeking* God's Word so much as *becoming* God's Word. We become the living, radiant incarnation of God's own compassion, long-suffering, and fearless love. At that point we literally become God's Word of Assurance for others.

Inside each one of our hearts, then, God's Spirit has two "phases." Either it seeks God's Word or it welcomes God's Word. Either it presses a question or it enjoys an answer. It is the two phases of love. In the first phase, love is *eros,* love as concern, love that seeks the means to a beloved end. In the second phase, love is *agape,* love as appreciation, love that possesses its beloved and overflows in benevolence.

Corresponding to these two phases of the heart, there are two phases of human meaning. They are, first, the meanings that address our hearts and stimulate wonder there. I'm thinking, for example, of the meaning of suffering, of humor, of sex, of all the wisdom in our tradition that presents itself to us through our parents and homeland, and of all the meanings of the Gospel proclamation insofar as these raise questions in us.

Then there are the meanings our hearts embrace.

These are not only the meanings which we carry in thought but pre-eminently those which we embody in action for all to see. They include our attitudes towards suffering, humor, sex, tradition, and the Gospel.

It is our attitude towards the Gospel that gives the saving key to all the rest. By embracing the Gospel as the heart's saving truth, we embody the humanly divine meanings of God himself. We become, with Jesus at our head, the Body of Christ, the fulness of God's Logos.

In one sense, this is very familiar stuff. Many of the great saints were converted on account of the powerful witness of Gospel men and women. We too, we who have never laid eyes on Jesus, believe that we truly "receive" him through the Christian community. And let's not be ashamed to admit that our efforts to live out the Gospel have been edifying for others. I have found that at those times when I feel least resourceful for helping others because life has ground me down, then God providentially sends someone my way who asks me for help in the one thing I have left: trust in God. That divine poverty must show on my face.

In another sense, while we can admit that our lives have at least some effect on one another, it's going quite a bit further to act on the firm belief that we are God's own incarnation — not because divinity is ours by right, of course, but because we are Assured of being God's Assurance to the world. A lamp ought not be hidden under a basket, Jesus said. We are to let our light shine before others, confident that every day our faces grow brighter and brighter as we are turned into the one whose image we reflect.

When we pray in the first phase, the phase of addressing God and being addressed by God, our prayer has the quality of an unfinished dialogue. Our hearts bear a wonder, that we are restless to resolve, or else the Gospel challenges us to a conversion deeper than we have experienced so far. This is the hungry, restless, longing phase of prayer.

When we pray in the second phase, the phase of togetherness and resting with God's Assurance, our prayer is a more silent and massive presence. Our hearts have found their beloved, not only in a mystical embrace, but in the flesh and blood of Jesus contemplated in very earthy settings and carried into our own place and time through loving our neighbor.

Prayer, then, belongs to the core of any and every genuine human progress. Its two phases are discernible in all true development — in those strivings that instigate change for the better and in those resolutions that consolidate those changes.

Not all this "prayer" is explicit, of course. But everything in the unfolding of human history belongs to the Spirit's groaning and praying when we cannot find words. Explicit prayer is the bringing into the open before God whatever movements, crises, agreements, and yearnings happen to make up the slice of history that we each call our story. In our next chapter I hope to show how this emerging history, with prayer at its core, finds its perfection in meeting God. But for now, we still have to complete our reflections on God's Word.

THIS vision of how we raise our minds and hearts to God — that is, of how we pray — is incomplete not only because our understanding is partial but also in another, more tragic sense. For although our souls have the desire and the means to embrace all they truly need, the outrageous truth is that our poor souls refuse.

This bewilders us to death.

Why, pray tell, if our minds and hearts know how to find God, do they repeatedly quit their search? Why do we side-track our genuine prayer by refusing to admit it's prayer? Why do we let ourselves get all mucked-up in compromises? How in the world did we ever reach that impass in which we felt we had no choice but to go it alone? Oh, why do we refuse to come home, when the distance is short and we well know the way?

One might say that we do not trust, or that we prefer to live without God, but that just restates the problem in more general terms. No doubt, we do not trust God as we ought. But why not?

Because we are afraid, some say.

Well, of course we are afraid. We are afraid of letting go of control over our lives. We are afraid to risk, afraid to love, afraid to pressure other people for what we believe is their own good.

Fear is certainly at the root of all our real problems. And what are we afraid of? It may seem as though we are afraid of God, afraid of facing the You behind everything, afraid of the uncanny invitation he makes to become a We with him. There's some truth to this, but it too quickly overlooks a prior truth about ourselves which, if we accept it, has the power to make us quake like any single-minded mystic.

The prior truth I'm referring to is the fact that *we are afraid of what we ourselves might do.*

A married man falls in love with the woman he works with. He wants to stay faithful to his wife, but let us suppose that he has opportunity, desire, and invitation to have an affair. Were such a man to cheat on his wife, isn't it usually because at some point he thinks to himself, "I don't know how long I can keep myself from this; I'm afraid that sooner or later I'm going to give in."

Put like that, doing wrong sounds like a matter of facing the facts — here, the "fact" that eventually he will give in to the temptation.

But that's not a fact at all. It's only a possibility — but a possibility he is afraid of. In this confusion he resembles the way each of us faces what bedevils us. We are afraid of being doomed to do wrong. Not wrong in general, but wrong in one very particular area where we feel helpless and alone.

Our fear blazes up fueled by this ambiguity: Are we really helpless and alone or not? Yes or no?

Allow me to press the question on you more directly: Don't respond that you *feel* helpless and alone. The question is *Are* you? Don't drone on about how difficult it is for you to understand how a spiritual God could possibly be present to a creature of flesh and blood. The question is, *Is* he? Don't waste your time telling yourself how evil and selfish you are and unworthy of anything so good as God's help and company. Does God help you or not? Is he there or not? Yes or no?

This is the act of faith. It's answering Yes or No to whether God is trustworthy, whether he is there Assuring us from within and from without that our hearts can find their quarry. Is the Lord very near or not? Is there any need to worry or not?

Whether we answer Yes or whether we answer No, we bring to reality the answer we give, and all evidence thereafter only supports our judgment. If I say, "I am alone and God cannot help me avoid wrong," then I become alone and God indeed cannot help me avoid wrong. But if I say, "God can help me avoid wrong," or, as it more likely comes out, "*You* can help me avoid wrong," then God can and does in fact help.

What sort of person says to God, "Yes, You can help"? Only the person who receives God's Double Assurance where he or she feels helpless — the person who not only loves God but lets that love conquer, through the here and now, the ancient fear that one is destined to fail as a human being.

Let's not forget how well we know this feeling of being destined to doing wrong and what a great front of bravado we put up when we let that feeling smother what faith reveals. We swallow the desperate look on our faces and speak with great conviction and strut around with an air of high purpose — while making victims out of persons we refuse to look in the face.

I've seen it in people who Xerox reams of copy-righted music, acting as though it's the only sensible thing to do. I've read about it in reliable accounts of corporation presidents who take pride in the clever way they keep workers from organizing by fueling racial hatred among them. (A big difference in scale there? Certainly — but no difference in the pattern. And it's the small-scale pattern that presents itself as a ready solution to big-scale moral conflicts.)

It's the profoundest lie we know: thinking we are unassured, we act self-assured, while real Assurance presses upon our souls from within and from without. But what an act it is!

In our hearts we know who we are. The Genesis account of the Fall tells our story: "The eyes of both of them were opened and they realized they were naked." What did they know in knowing they were naked? There was certainly nothing wrong in *being* naked, for naked they were in their time of innocence. The shame cannot be on account of nakedness. The shame lay rather in how — not in what — they knew.

To put it simply: They knew by themselves.

They reached a truth outside of God's company. Exegetes today generally believe that this is the meaning of the story that our first parents ate from the Tree of the Knowledge of Good and Evil: that from the beginning, we wanted to decide right and wrong on our own. No doubt, on our own we have learned a few things about good and evil, but it's such narrow truths that make up the broadest lies. The eyes of Adam and Eve were truly opened; they did see some difference between right and wrong; but they came to themselves all by themselves.

So: "When the man and his wife heard the sound of the Lord God walking in the Garden in the cool of the day, they hid from the Lord among the trees of the Garden." From that day right up to our own, there is the possibility of self-commitment and self-knowledge divorced from God.

This means that we have the capacity to do good and to reach the truth outside of the space in which we and God gaze on each other. Not that God doesn't give that capacity, but that we can exercise it as though we were alone. Think, for example, of our habit of wondering how we're doing. We're checking up on ourselves. We do it in the name of virtue, perfection, goodness, whatever — but it is we that do it.

We ought to be ashamed of ourselves. In the encounter with God we need not fear our nakedness. He loves what he sees so much that all introspection and self-analysis on our part alone is an outrage to him.

It has always been a principle of the life of the Spirit that one can never know one's sin except in the experience of the light of God's forgiveness. We are not called first to know our own sin and then bring it to God for forgiveness. No, our primeval call is simply to join God in the Garden, in the cool of the day. There is no valid self-knowledge outside that walk with him.

This is the original sin. We want goodness without God. We hide our nakedness and traipse around in fig leaves of pretended confidence. But we are all naked underneath. And in that nakedness, whether we admit it or not, we fear that we might choose to destroy our own integrity. We might. So we go ahead and do it. Insane. Utterly stupid.

We have chosen death again, inheritors of the Fall that we are. Not the death in which we stop breathing, but the far more tragic and ever-looming death in which we stop trusting God. The authors of Genesis were so overwhelmed by the horror of this human autonomy that they regarded physical death as its natural consequence. We die because we are already dead in our self-centeredness.

Were there no clear word of Assurance from without that we need not fear, we might be excused. But the Good News of Jesus divides those who hear it into the liberated and the condemned. It declares who is alive and who is dead. Assurance is there to make that difference.

ON the other side of our imagined destiny in evil, we also imagine ourselves as incapable of most of the good in our world that begs doing. For example, consider the effect on your compassion of the following account recently published by a news agency — the sort of report we regularly read in our newspapers:

> "Refugees staggering into Thailand from Cambodia are painting a picture of people dying like flies in their war-ravaged homeland, relief officials said here yesterday.

> "Officials said recent arrivals in Thailand included babies who were just 'skin and bones,' adults who were living skeletons and many people suffering from malnutrition, malaria and diarrhea.
>
> "'These people tell that as they walk through the forests toward Thailand, they see bodies lying everywhere,' one official said.
>
> "Reports from relief, diplomatic and other sources available here yesterday spoke of a heavy daily death toll in malaria-infested areas across the border where very little food and medicine is available."

Compassion doesn't come sailing out so readily, does it? It's not as quick as when we hear of, say, one small child slamming a door on his finger. Compassion must be under a Law of Inertia all its own. It seems to take on the weight of the matter it responds to. Thus, it starts quickly in light matters and leadenly in heavy matters.

I don't believe we can acquit our compassion of having failed us on the big problems by saying that such problems are not part of our experience. We can begin to experience such problems merely by going to an evening's talk given by people involved, watching their slides, reading up on the background of the problems or becoming familiar with the people and agencies that are trying to do something about them. There is no mystique about persons who suffer from socio-economic disasters, nor about those better-off persons who have let themselves become concerned. We can meet them; and we usually find ordinary persons like ourselves.

However, we know damned well that such initial

exposures have the power to move us, and that the Law of Inertia will show its corollary: Weighty compassion set in motion will tend to stay in motion. In other words, once we let our concern loose on the bigger issues, it's liable to carry us we know not where.

Again we find ourselves afraid of what we might do, only this time, instead of feeling doomed to mess up where we feel helpless and alone, we feel doomed to do good.

Doomed to do good — and we are afraid of it.

Certainly we all have some good reason for our fear. We are afraid of getting into something we lack the resources for, to say nothing of simply being afraid of the tedium and weariness exacted by social concern. We can legitimately say that our time is limited, or our money. We can legitimately assess our particular allotments of emotional and intellectual resources. Fair enough.

But no one of us knows, either by past experience or by rational assessment of one's capacities, just how much goodness he or she is capable of. It's our spiritual resources which quite possibly have no limit — the ability to put the needs of others before our own, the endurance to hang in there under the pressure of the malice of others, the working belief that risky compassion beats secure isolation any day of the week.

Even if we do accept unlimited goodness as an ideal, we still fear to act on it in particular ways. We know that God's gentle push within us towards goodness will lead us to a life-style shaped far more by the needs of others than by our own autonomous choices. We are afraid, in short, of becoming good in ways determined by the predicaments of people we can reach out to. We'd rather stick with being good within fixed and familiar boundaries.

Again, we find ourselves wanting goodness without God, goodness with our fence around it. Our heart assures us from within that being good has no limit, and God's Word from without assures us that reaching out may be crucifying at times, but it never deals out death.

The death at the end of our lives stands like an Avenging Angel, not announcing for each one that the time to die has come, but announcing for each one whether he or she is already dead or not. That Angel belongs to Jesus, who proclaims that the death at the end of our lives is no more to be feared than the deaths of our own autonomy during our lives — deaths we underwent whenever we accepted the Double Assurance of God's Spirit and his Gospel.

4
MEETING GOD

THIS morning I rolled out of bed, showered, dressed, and sat down to breakfast. I enjoy a cup of coffee and an English muffin with peanut butter on it. I especially love peanut butter. It has the nearly metaphysical properties of prime matter: breakfast would be insubstantial without it, and an insubstantial breakfast makes for an insubstantial day. I thank God for it and I hope there will be peanut butter in heaven — or at least something of its delicious essence.

I can't believe that in heaven God is going to do away with the things we dearly love. Somehow, nothing worthwhile will be lost.

Let's take some time here to let our imaginations of heaven play a bit. "Heaven" has always stood not just for a life after this one, but for a life that completes this one — and God knows, this life is painfully incomplete. All believers, young and old, see behind the pearly gates marvels fashioned directly from their own experience of incompleteness on earth. So it might help to deepen our understanding of how we pray to God here and now if we imagine what meeting him in heaven is going to be like.

When I was a child, I was confident I knew exactly what heaven would be like: plenty of sunshine and plenty of fun. Later, as my own notion of happiness enlarged, I came to believe that heaven would mean all humankind united in loving and praising God. I still believe that. But I have become more skeptical about the adequacy of human words to anticipate meeting God, and at the same time more sanguine about the foreshadowings of that meeting which we already enjoy. I can now envision a heaven in startling continuity with life as it comes on earth.

Imagine that after we die, rather than going through some door to a new, delightful place, we undergo an uncanny "fold" in both time and space, so that we do not experience anything new at all. No new data, no new sights or sounds. Rather, imagine that we experience in a single moment all the experiences of every single moment of our own lives — not experiencing them a *second* time, as though life were some videotape to be replayed but, through a space-time "fold," experiencing them truly for the first time. It would be like taking an end-view of our life's time line, so that we experience it all as a single point.

The only difference — the huge difference — is that now we understand unambiguously what our experiences mean. Now we know exactly when and where and with whom are hearts are true.

For one thing, we will understand how constantly and how intensely we pray. Not always on our knees, certainly, and not necessarily with the word "God" on our lips, but, respecting "something assuring" with a humble awe, we wordlessly trust our restlessness within and the Gospel from without. There is so much praise going on here that in this "folded" heaven, new acts of praise may not be necessary.

Further, we will understand clearly what Jesus meant when he said, "Philip, to have seen me is to have seen the Father." We will realize that Jesus is the perfect revelation of God, with nothing missing, nothing hidden, nothing superfluous. Jesus in the flesh. (Yes, the flesh: the reason why the early Church stressed the bodily resurrection of Jesus is to impress on us that the eternal Word of God bears an irrevocably human nature. Jesus did not "go back" to being divine, leaving human messiness behind.) So the moments when we turn to Jesus and the Gospel for guidance will shine like the sun in our lives. These are the moments when we truly find God.

We will also understand clearly Jesus' words, "As long as you did it to the least of my brothers and sisters, you did it to me." We will see Jesus in the flesh in all those people we care for. We will not meet Jesus in the way that we meet someone we've heard about but never met. It will be more like the solution scene in a comedy in which a man and a woman whose paths have criss-crossed in countless ways recognize one another as long-lost brother and sister. For Jesus is not *disguised* as poor, naked, hungry, wandering, or imprisoned. Rather, persons who are poor, naked, hungry, wandering, or imprisoned *reveal* him in a way nothing else earthly can.

This heaven that is made up exclusively with earth's

data will be an embarrassing surprise. The surprise will not be because of things new and fascinating, but because we will know the living God and he will look startlingly human and familiar. What we call "Purgatory" may be nothing but the degree of our painful embarrassment over not having recognized God earlier.

Finally, we will know hell, too. We will see clearly that hell is not a place of punishment for some crime. Hell is refusing to cooperate with the prayer going on within us. Hell is turning a deaf ear to the whisperings of one's own wonder and consequently missing altogether the gift in life as it comes. In other words, hell is the deliberate rejection of Assurance.

Think of the Prodigal Son's older brother. He was offered everything by his father — "Everything I have is yours" — but somewhere along the line he chose to receive only what he could earn. He simply lost taste for accepting Assurance freely and lovingly given. I think this is far more terrifying an account of hell than all the descriptions of weeping and gnashing of teeth. It's terrifying because you and I have stood at this hell's threshold every time we preferred self-assurance over dependence on God. Once our very desire for Assurance is buried under self-assurance, even our wonder lacks the power to resurrect itself.

I have asked you to imagine all this. But will heaven really look this way? Nobody knows. Imagination can raise questions about the truth, and imagination can gather a set of truths into a symbolic whole but imagination is not knowledge of the truth. The purpose of this exercise in imagination is really to ask a yes-or-no question about the truth of things.

Is it true or not that our experiences of our own selves and our own traditions contain trustworthy data on God as he really is? That is, is the real "God" truly known through wonder embracing the Word? Will not the knowledge we gain this way on earth be an irreplaceable part of the knowledge we will have in "heaven"?

And is it true or not that there is no other way of knowing God except by letting this Double Assurance do its work in us — no gnostic secret that contemplatives or gurus keep to themselves, no vision giving a peek to privileged saints. When the mystics among us complain that they cannot put into words what they have seen of God, are they under any other limitation than the limitation we all feel when we speak of someone who loves us?

If there is some way other than wonder embracing the Word, some way accessible only to the few, then all of us, including those special few, should stifle all our questions and lay a firm quietus upon our hearts. Or if, in God's private calculus of salvation, wonder's effort to embrace the Word effects some completely unfathomable change in our souls, we still would have no way of understanding it or cooperating with it intelligently.

If, on the other hand, there is no alternate route than our own wonder, and no salvation from the fear that wonder encounters except through the Gospel, then God takes our humanity seriously, particularly the two movements that make each one of us the human being that he or she is — the special, even pecular path that our lifelong wonder has traced, and the special, even peculiar transformations that the Gospel has demanded.

Within these two movements and only in the meeting of these two movements do we meet the real God.

We truly meet him here and now. Not perfectly, certainly, because something terrifyingly awesome in God seems to demand that our embrace be consummated only in the long crunch of humiliations, sufferings, and death and will not be completed until every living thing has submitted. But the Word of God which our particular wonder now resonates with will echo forever. Not a single word of God returns to him empty without carrying out what it was sent to do.

RIGHT here we seem to be on the verge of wondering what it will be like to see God face-to-face. But there's something else we do when we pray which we haven't mentioned yet; something rather obvious, but something which, if we reflect on it in the manner in which we have been reflecting on prayer already, will reveal a breadth to God's presence that narrow expressions like "face-to-face" tend to overlook.

The obvious phenomenon is this: we pray for people. We find ourselves praying that a relative in the hospital gets better, praying for sunshine on a free weekend, praying for the people who hold religious and political office and have to make decisions that will affect our lives.

I'm not saying that we "ought" to pray for people. We just do. It's natural for persons who love God to bring their concerns for others to him.

We don't even have to think of it as praying. Whenever we not only wish that things would work out for the best but also trust that they will, we are counting on "something assuring." When we say to a heart-sick friend, "Don't worry; things will work out," we give that reassurance not just because it will calm them down, but because we also believe it to be true. Everything will in fact "work out."

But even though we all find ourselves praying for others in this way, we don't all understand what it is we are doing. Often we conceive it in a way that is counter-productive to anticipating what meeting God is going to involve.

For instance, many people have constructed for themselves a world view that grants God the right to intervene in his own game on his own behalf — as though he were running an illegal roulette wheel in which he can, by covert manipulation, make the little ball drop into a groove favorable to the house. In this scheme it makes plenty of sense to ask for special considerations. The trouble is that such a God can be paid off, usually with the currency of "prayers and sacrifices," and in the long run nobody really trusts such a Wheeler-Dealer God.

Besides, in this view of things, we take our own

measures of "better" and "worse" far too seriously. We decide independently of God what seems good for others and then sidle up to his table with a deal in mind. Are we really expecting to meet such a God at life's end?

Another counter-productive way of thinking about intercessory prayer is to spend all our time wondering how it works. We ponder how the silent prayer of one person could possibly effect a change in the life of another. The underlying assumption here is that prayer is some sort of invisible push, and that God works exclusively through pushing people around. Such a view distorts the nature of God's presence to us both now and in eternity. Even if we cite cases of how prayer brought about marvelous healings, or even if we acknowledge the clairvoyant and psychokinetic powers, which preturnatural persons of all cultures seem to possess, we seem more anxious to maintain prayer's power than God's power. How psychic communication works is a problem for psychological research. What we who do pray for people want to know is rather what our God is like who creates persons with a natural bent towards praying for one another.

To understand what God is like, we have to begin with the raw data provided by the spontaneous movement of our spirit — here, the spirit that finds itself praying for others.

Here's a homey example of that movement. My father, who was almost completely bald, was bending over some celery he was cutting up for a salad one evening. I was there in the kitchen, and I saw directly above him the cabinet door slowly swing open like a weapon moving into strike position. In that quick moment, I saw it all ahead of time. But I couldn't warn him; to shout "Look out!" would have prompted him to jerk his head up for sure. But jerk up he did, whacking his shiney bald head hard into the stubborn corner of the door.

"Ouch!" I cried.

My "Ouch!" was louder than my father's "Ouch!"

And didn't you say some sort of mental "Ouch!" too?

You don't even know my father and yet you felt for him much the way I did. I don't know whether praying for other people has any statistically measurable effect on their lives outside of the more tangible ways we might care for them. But I do know that in each one of us the spirit of wonder is ready to cry "Ouch!" over the pain of any other. No matter how delighted we might feel on a given day, the news of the misfortune of others can temper our delight with solicitude, provided we let our spirit feel for others.

Wonder, that spirit that tests all things and demands the best of all things, that spirit that would soar to heaven rather than rest in any one thing, is tethered to the earth by compassion. We are creatures with a single, shared spirit. You cry "Ouch!" over my father's pain, much as I might cry "Hooray!" over your good fortune. It's as though a single spirit of wonder borrows tongue somewhere or other to utter its elemental cry.

The question is, when we let wonder loose on spontaneous compassion, are we distracting ourselves from our real goal, which is to encounter the living God? Earlier I said that wonder asks to be trusted that it will find what it is looking for. But wonder does not peer so intently at its far horizon that it overlooks the ordinary needs of humanity at hand. Wonder reads the morning paper, answers the phone, listens intently to any story that is human.

We trust the part of our hearts which will not rest until it rests in the "You" it longs for. Now our hearts ask us to trust the other part which gets side-tracked by the sight of a man or a woman or a child in trouble.

It seems to me that if we can count on our natural spirit of compassion now, we can count on it in "heaven," when all our "nows" are gathered into one. That spirit, which unites us in spontaneous concern for one another at the same time that it calls us into a dark future alone, still will not allow us to come before God in single file. We would all be looking over our shoulders for the others. We want to enter, not just "face-to-face," but as "family-to-family."

In short, the heart's way to God permanently includes the heart's diversion towards the neighbor. We are Assured of that from within.

We are Assured of that from without, too. A friend of mine likes to ask people to fill in the blank in this line from the First Epistle of John:

My friends, if God has so loved us,
then we also ought to love __________.

To love whom? God? No, the text reads, "then we also ought to love one another."

The logic here is the logic of family pride. We honor our family name not so much by returning our parents' love as by spreading it around. Those rare families and religious communities that seem to have a dynastic grip on the Spirit of God seem also to be possessed by a Spirit of Compassion.

That Spirit obviously possessed Jesus. While the vertical component in his wonder cried, "Father, protect those you have given to me," the horizontal component cried, "Come to me all you who labor and are heavily burdened, and I will give you rest." In other words, while Jesus did pray for people, he also acted on their behalf. He acted with the Assurance that the compassion he rendered was the very compassion of the loving God of us all.

When the Spirit of Compassion ignites our wonder in the direction of our neighbor, we should be careful to be attentive to that wonder's two phases. We not only address God on behalf of others, we also act for others with the Assurance that we embody God's compassion. Or, to put it very practically, instead of simply praying, "Lord, give your comfort to Uncle Joe in this time of trial," we might pray, "Lord, choose us to be your comfort to Uncle Joe; give us the wisdom to speak encouraging words and to act with the peace of your Assurance."

THE "Beatific Vision." The expression originally denoted a clear apprehension of God by means of one's spirit, not by one's eye. Nowadays, since literally it means a "happy sight," it has come to connote the happiness that comes from looking on the beautiful sight of God. But God does not consider himself "over there" to be looked at any more than a person you or I love does.

Suppose for a moment that you were to be involved in a serious automobile accident and that, as a result of head injuries, you were to lose your sight. Imagine yourself in a hospital bed, aching from your injuries, aching from the operation on your eyes, but aching mainly from the searing loneliness brought on by the prospect of being blind for the rest of your life.

Then, footsteps "Is that you?" you ask, hoping for one of those certain people whose company is good hot soup for the soul.

"Hi. It's me," she says (or he, depending).

"Ah . . . ah!" goes the heart.

In the upsailing of the heart, taking a look is not essential. The essential is the question, "Is that you? Are you there?"

"You — you whom my heart seeks. Are you there? I don't need to *look;* I want to *know."*

So goes the question pressed by all those who know that staying alive is a painful and often lonely struggle.

Let's not call it the Beatific Vision. Let's call it the Beatific Welcome.

What will that welcome be like? Images of God

enthroned, in commanding appearance, stay stuck in the vision of our minds like old photos we stuck in the corners of our mirrors long ago. And like those old photos, our early images haven't been noticed much lately, unless someone asks.

We are asking now. But there's no need to pull out the old photos. We can look there in the mirror at ourselves. In our own persons we will see the primary evidence on what that welcome will be. It is precisely the sorts of welcome we seem made for. After all, if God is Assurance, he cannot have planted in us a hope for a welcome we will never enjoy.

What sorts of welcome do we long for? If we can prescind from all our cultural difference, I think we can discern two basic sorts of welcome — welcomes that complement one another. First there is your welcome for me: a welcome between an I and a Thou, in which each focuses on and appreciates the other. Afterwards, once I and Thou have embraced, there is our welcome together for the "We" we are becoming. We are focused not so much on one another as on the community that we are.

A wedding, for example, celebrates the I-Thou welcome: wife and husband in mutual love. On the tenth anniversary of their wedding, the same couple celebrates the union they have become: a We-Us welcome. Not that the welcome between I and Thou ever flags. It flourishes as I and Thou become a single welcomer for the communion which is more than I or Thou alone.

If this evidence of the heart is any Assurance of the

Beatific Welcome, then in that welcome there will be not only a loving greeting between God and us. There will also be a common welcome by God and us for the community we make together. We are Assured of this from within.

There's Assurance for this two-fold welcome from without, too, in the Word we can trust. Jesus not only addressed countless persons as an I to a Thou. Upon those who became his disciples, he breathed his own Spirit and they went out, not away from Jesus, but in the power of Jesus, curing and preaching in his name. There is not a shred of evidence in the entire New Testament that anyone hankered after The-Good-Old-Days-Gone-By which they had with Jesus. Jesus was not a matter of the past tense and old haunts. Every day had become, shall we say, The-Good-New-Day-Going-On that they enjoyed in his company.

The Beatific Welcome, then, will include sharing in Jesus' own gladness of spirit. Not only will we be welcomed into the company of Jesus, we will join Jesus in doing that welcoming ourselves. The Spirit who does the welcoming in us will do a double leap for joy: joy over God as "Thou" and joy over the Body of Christ as "Us."

If that's the way "heaven" is going to be, then it's too bad that we don't let ourselves enjoy more this second sort of welcome while on earth. We should let ourselves walk *with* Jesus instead of imagining that we're pursuing him in some cavernous spiritual forest. We Christians are not the Hounds of Heaven; Christ is the Hound and he trots at our side.

We're timid, though. Or perhaps "cautious" is the word. We pretend to be unworthy to speak and act in his name, as though to avoid being caught by God in evil unawares. But God's "name" belongs to us. We are a "We" with God and act in "our" name. It is not even too presumptious to say that when others reject us because of who we are, they reject Christ. When Paul was persecuting Christians, Jesus said, "Why do you persecute *me?"*

In short, then, the Beatific Welcome will contain both kinds of welcome. Human love never tires of either, and the perfect love which the Gospel reports has both, too. The Good News is both something we receive and something we become, and this is an eternal fact of life.

YOU may have noticed the similarity between these two modes of welcome and what we earlier called the two phases of prayer. This is no coincidence, for the two modes of welcome are the perfection of those two phases of prayer. In that prayer, you recall, there is the phase of mutual address, in which wonder and Word address one another, and there is the phase of togetherness, in which wonder and Word embrace. Even on earth, in the prayer of mutual address, we speak with God as I and Thou. Let no one convince us that such a prayer is sheerly a reaching for what we cannot touch until heaven; were God's Spirit not already in our hearts praying, we couldn't even begin to wonder.

And the prayer of togetherness, too, in which our wonder cherishes the Word of the Gospel and becomes an incarnation of that Word, has its rightful place on earth. Let no one convince us that God does not share his divine nature with us when we embody the Word of the Gospel in our everyday lives.

Prayer, then, is the eternal core of our being. It is the core of our history, as we saw, because it brings to the divine interpersonal sphere all the strivings of history and all its true achievements. Prayer is also the means by which each of us beats death and discovers life. And finally, prayer is the action that carries us through death and blossoms into a two-fold Beatific Welcome. In that blossoming, nothing of value will be missing — not any noble deed, no hidden heroism, and, no, not even peanut butter.

It might be wise at this point to draw a diagram outlining the structure of prayer — the core of history and our rehearsal for heaven. It will clear up some confusion, perhaps, between Double Assurance and the two phases of prayer. It will also set the context for stating what the Trinitarian foundations of prayer are, which we will take up immediately afterwards.

	Two Phases of Prayer	
	Mutual Address	Togetherness
Assurance from within	Spirit within our wonder seeking the Word	Spirit within our wonder appreciating the Word
Assurance from without	Word of Jesus addressing our lives	Word of Jesus incarnated in our lives

The left-hand column, "Mutual Address," depicts the kind of prayer in which either we are seeking the heart's "You" or the Gospel is challenging our hearts. It's an I-Thou relationship. The right-hand column, "Togetherness," depicts the prayer of joy, of appreciation, of confirmation over the love that binds us together with God — a We-Us relationship.

In each phase of prayer, God's Double Assurance is at work. When, in the first phase, we seek the Lord, we enjoy an *a priori* Assurance both that our hearts will not rest until they rest in the "You" they seek and that the Gospel reveals this "You" for our time and place. When, in the second phase, we find the Lord and embrace his will, sharing his purposes with him, we feel the inner Assurance of a happy wonder that has found the Good News, and we become the outer Assurance for others by embodying the Gospel in our lives.

This prayer may be implicit or explicit. It is implicit when we focus on the horizontal component of our rising wonder — the problems that face us, the stars that elicit awe from us, the decisions we have to make about our responsibilities. It is explicit when we focus on the vertical component — that is, when we turn to the "You" we love either in mutual address or in joint welcome over the glory we make together.

In heaven, we say, there is no time. We do not move from one state to another. One might expect that one of these two phases of prayer has to collapse into the other; and the first phase seems the likely candidate. Yet remember that this first phase represents a kind of loving that most of us would rather not see absorbed —

the direct love between I and Thou. If this inkling of our hearts carries the weight of Assurance that it seems to, then we simply have to postulate two forms of "welcome" in heaven, without saying whether one follows after the other.

WE have been talking about our meeting with God. We have found that, if God really is Doubly Assuring for us, then our experiences of love give us clues about eternal realities. In particular, we found that the structure of our prayer and our historical process in time is the very structure of our meeting God in eternity. And if we remember that "eternity" refers to an existence which is not *after* time but which encompasses our very present time, then the reality of our prayer is the reality of our meeting God. It is no mere rehearsal.

Now let us talk about God as he is in himself. The God of our experience may be the God we meet; that is, meeting God in eternity may make sense out of all human experience. But we can still ask whether the God we meet this way really is God-in-himself. For example, might there turn out to be more than three persons in God? Could the one we call the Holy Spirit just as easily have become human? (If so, then the fact that the Holy Spirit works through human wonder does not reveal anything absolute about God in himself.)

To both such questions, we have to answer No, if

Assurance is real. There can be no more persons in God than the persons we know of. Our experience of the Spirit really is data on God-in-himself. And the rock-bottom "proof" of these doctrines is not some logical analysis, but the living fact of Double Assurance working in us who ask.

If anyone wanted to "prove" that God is doubly processing (and therefore, Source, Word and Spirit), or if anyone wanted to repeat the process by which our spiritual ancestors came to know this, one would only have to begin with the saving dogma that in Jesus of Nazareth God has really given us Assurance of his saving love.

Our own spirit of wonder will not let go of that outer Assurance; we will press it as far as it will bear; we will bring up before the Paschal mystery both our sin and our death to see if Assurance Saves us there. And the more we probe our belief in Jesus, the more we become aware that our probing itself is Assurance from within. That is, in accepting Jesus as our Assurance in the face of deaths, we realize that the Spirit of wonder which pursued that Good News has been a divine, Assuring gift as well.

I want to avoid saying that therefore we came to know God as "Trinity," even though we eventually did. Over a hundred years before that term was used, Christians experienced God as doubly self-giving. Irenaeus, for example, spoke of God's "two hands." If the term "dogma" refers to those doctrines that are saving, then the absolutely central Chrstian dogma on God is that he has a saving Word to speak and a Spirit of welcome for that Word.

We know this about God. He has "revealed" it through the religious spirit of humankind and the religious Word that Jesus of Nazareth becomes for those who have received it. That doesn't mean that he "told" us what he was like. As we said, the method itself was Assurance. He planted his own doubly-processing self into the soil of humanity, becoming the Spirit of welcome within our spirits and the Word of Assurance within our history.

From the living experience of Double Assurance, it was natural to wonder about God-in-himself, although this is quite a specialized kind of question. It is similar to the insight that occurred to the Israelites sometime during the second millenium B.C. as they shifted from what we call "henotheism" to "monotheism." It dawned on them that their one god is really *the* God. They moved from a belief in *a* single god to a belief in *the* God who is the "true" God. And I can remember a high school junior's question for religion class: "Father, is our God the real God?" Like many of us, that student grew up knowing what he believed, but not knowing whether it was true.

It is true, then, that the real God has two processions, an outer procession of self-expression and an inner procession of self-welcome. This is the "self" of God, regardless of whether he created anything. This is the God every living person is restless for: the "Unknown God" to some and the God of mystical love to others. This is the God who watches over us as we sleep, the all-present yet ever-beyond God. There is none but him.

For hundreds and hundreds of years since Christ, it has been said that we cannot understand these two processions except by analogy, because no created analog can be an adequate model for the essence of God. Still, we can at least "point." We can say that the Jesus of our history is the very one we will know as the eternal Logos in God. And the Spirit of Love by which we love God is the very one we will know as the eternal Spirit of God.

The God we encounter in the Beatific Welcome, then, will be the God of our experience. We will "know" the Holy Spirit through our own lifetime of being driven by restless wonder and joy over truth and goodness where we embraced it. There is nothing that suggests that this mode of knowing the Spirit will radically change, as if we will suddenly be able to take a good look at some unusual bird.

We will "know" the eternal Word not only through all the horizontal instances of it that challenged us and challenged others through us — all the truly significant and worthwhile events, all the truly selfless men and women — but pre-eminently in the person of Jesus, who unambiguously incarnated true life in a world beset by ambiguity and sin.

We will "know" God as Source precisely as source of the Christ-like self-giving love we witnessed in life and the self-transcending love that impelled our own human hearts to seek their source.

This "knowing" God will be not three acts, but one. It will be something like the way we "know" the families we grew up in. This is because within our own consciousness of our last names we know ourselves as bearing a family spirit, as representing that family, and as receiving our values from parents and grand-parents.

I have been using English words, some derived from Latin systematic theology and some from Continental existentialism. But here, where we are trying to affirm a saving dogma, the words are not that important. What is important is the inner acts of judgment that what our words represent is really so — that the Doubly Assuring God of our experience is truly a doubly-processing, absolutely universal ground of all things.

THIS brings us, finally, to a doctrine about ourselves which, I guarantee, will light up your face with a permanent look of happy surprise. It's an ancient doctrine — the early Fathers of the Church saw it clearly — and yet it has been neglected in our tradition time and time again.

Perhaps you have already seen it. Have you noticed the startling similarity between God and us? God has two ways within himself for being his best self — by uttering his love and by welcoming the love he utters. And we, as a three-million-year-old community of women and men, have a similar way of becoming our best selves — by uttering love through meaningful action and by welcoming in love the real value of those actions.

Who are we then? We are the possibility of God giving himself outside of himself. No less than that and no more than that either. The reason we are made shapeable by the lifetime of our questions playing upon the range of situations and persons that present themselves to us is precisely so that we can receive God's own self in a Double Assurance. The idea of humanity was not just an idea God plucked out of an indefinitely deep hat of possible worlds. He drew the idea from his own doubly-processing self. We are nothing but the possibility of welcoming God as he really is.

The Genesis doctrine that we are made in the image and likeness of God has taken on a brand-new profundity since Jesus laid down his life for his friends. We are made like God for the sole reason that as his Word and his Spirit operate in him, they might also operate in us, so that we can be a genuine community of love with God. The wonder that we spoke of in the second chapter, and the Word that we spoke of in the third, are the two "processions" within humanity that make it possible for God truly to give his own doubly-processing self to us. And in welcoming the Word, we become part of the community that is divine. We "share in the divinity of Christ, who emptied himself to share in our humanity."

THERE still remains far, far more to God. But if he is the lover he is reputed to be, then I am willing to bet that all the rest there is to know about God is already contained in the data on humanity. I am willing to bet that in the Beatific Welcome we will understand all the impenetrable familiarities we barely know how to question.

For example, last night I walked outside, and there it was, raining. Raining! I didn't expect it to rain. I wanted to go for a walk. God, why is there rain? Or, why are there mosquitoes?

There is no end to such questions: God, why are we creatures that need to sleep? Why do we nap and wake up grouchy? I'm not complaining, mind you, but having to sleep surely isn't just an arbitrary idea of yours, is it? Or, if we need to sleep in order to dream or rest or renew energy — that is, if sleep is a necessary part of growing — then why are we creatures that grow?

Why, indeed, are we creatures that fail to grow? Why is every Cain allowed to club his brother Abel?

Why are there so many of us spreading across this globe — apparently more of us than we can manage? Or, considering the hugeness of space, why so few of us by comparison? What is it of yourself that you give, letting us approach the mad possibility of annihilating every single one of ourselves?

And God, how I look forward to seeing why we are man and woman! Sex was your idea: a beautiful idea, universally evident in living things, powerfully preoccupying. But it cannot have been merely your whim, Ancient Friend. It has to be an incarnation of something sexual in you, if I may say so.

Come, Day of Yahweh! Come, beloved Raining and Walking, Mosquitoes, Sleep, Dreams! Come, Grouch; come, Time and Space; come, Freedom! Come, Sex; come, Friend!

5
LITURGICAL WORDS

WE have followed wonder's ascent in our soul and the entry of God's Word into our lives and found that we are nothing but wonder receiving Word — that every smidgen of meaning in our lives derives from that. Still, obviously, there is plenty of mystery left, and our analysis has to leave off where another kind of work must begin. We still have to hammer out the concrete meanings of "courage" or "self-confidence" or "social justice" in our lives. We still must actually find God, learn about him, become intimate with him through dedication to our neighbor. We still will never understand why we sin, since sin has no explanation, being utterly unintelligible. We still must live, even though the full meaning of life remains clouded in mystery.

If we have been emphasizing anything, we have emphasized that life is not obvious. Nor is death. It is not only for philosophers to wonder about such ultimates. Every person faces the unapologetic limitations of time, place, and culture that seem to confine a devouring inner thirst for life to its fullest. Every person feels the need for some intermediate haven where the absolutes of life can be embraced and, paradoxically, the limitations, too.

That's why, speaking very practically, wonder comes to liturgy.

This is not the place for a host of suggestions on how liturgies ought to be celebrated. It will be helpful, though, to illustrate briefly how liturgy — particularly Eucharistic liturgy — meets our need for words to hear and words to speak when "we cannot find words." My hope in this concluding chapter is that the "foundations of prayer" which we have found within ourselves will help locate liturgical prayer within our spirituality of Double Assurance.

ALL liturgy is a symbol. By that I mean liturgy is a set of images, sounds, smells, movements that gather our feelings and orient them in a specific direction. As a set of images, the liturgy stands for the ultimates of life and death, points to them, confronts us with them without attempting to analyze them. Liturgy is, in that sense, like a pair of tongs that enables us to hold the protean mystery in place for a moment before it changes shape, slips out of our grasp, and practically dares us to pick it up again.

The sights, sounds, smells, tastes, and movements of liturgy are meant to elicit our feelings about where real life and real death may lie in our lives. It is a school that teaches the delicate balance of affections and disaffections that ought to characterize a person who is really alive. In the midst of the world that identifies pleasure with value, and pain with evil, the liturgy teaches us to feel joy over painful self-sacrificing love, and to feel sorrow over pleasures that are merely self-indulgent. And in the midst of the world that thinks of humanity as an evolutionary accident, liturgy brings us into communion with our maker, our lover, our divine company.

The liturgy stands as a symbol between the sort of ideas we've talked about in this book and the actual self-deaths each of us is called to make when it comes to loving God and neighbor. It enables us to keep in touch with the mystery without either analyzing the life out of it or restricting its reach to a small corner of our lives.

The mystery has to do with life and death. Or, to put it more accurately, life *through* death. In the liturgy we call the Mass, the altar symbolizes the deaths in our lives. Yet these deaths are not like the slaughter of some yelping lamb under the knife of an Abraham. What long ago was an altar has become a dinner table, at which friends sit together and perceive in the meal the destruction of their autonomy through mutual love. So liturgy is an altar, but more than an altar. And liturgy is a dinner table, but more than a dinner table. It celebrates far more than the community symbolized by those who eat a meal together. It celebrates the community of those whose self-assurance is being relentlessly torn asunder and transformed into a received Assurance.

But the altar and the dinner table remain: chunks

of wood or stone that look like things we know, but all the while representing something we don't know fully. What we do there stands for the action of real life — whatever that may turn out to be. All we know is Christ Jesus and the power of his resurrection; and all we desire is to repeat the pattern of his death.

The two phases of prayer, which we saw latent in the very structure of human history and which anticipate the two modes of Beatific Welcome, are auspiciously evident in the Mass. In the Liturgy of the Word, we dialogue with God in mutual address: begging for mercy, hearing the challenge of the Gospel, and praying for those we love. In the Liturgy of the Eucharist, we join in God's own self-sacrificing action in the world by offering our everyday self-deaths in communion with the self-death of Jesus.

These two phases are also evident in the other sacramental rituals of Christian churches — baptism, confirmation, reconciliation, marriage, ordination, healing. In all these there is a phase of mutual address between God and us, followed by an action done in common by God and us together. We might imagine the two phases like this: God's Word arrives and then returns to him as an entire family with Jesus. The Word returns not as a mere echo but immensely amplified under the power of God's Spirit working in its receivers.

We shouldn't be surprised at this — that the structure which liturgy has taken on reflects the very structure of human history and presages the structure of eternity. Liturgy is the midwife that brings history into that life eternal, and the relentless concerns of human wonder have trained her well.

WE don't have to think a great deal about this at liturgy. We only have to do it, letting the symbol be an expression of that poignant and specific recent history of how wonder has stalked the Word in our lives.

Still, we do have to be careful not to let liturgy become perfunctory. Human history is a struggle between life and death. And it is no easy thing to tell the difference, as our reflections on wonder suggest. Unless we have a regular way of expressing that in-between-ness of our existence, we will smooth over the differences between real life and real death in ordinary situations. We will treat human ambiguities as sheer unconcern on God's part; and we will treat sin as mere mistake, something readily tolerable by God. Any liturgy in which we do not feel like steeplejacks in a high wind is a waste of time. No, worse than a waste of time. Robot-like liturgies become a symbol that true life is something quite obvious; and God, someone quite controllable.

All this can sound painfully ideal to the great majority of us who suffer through liturgies led by the incompetent. What an outrage they are to Christ, who gave his life so that we might be able to embrace life in all its mystery! I am ashamed of the way we have made attendance at liturgy a serious obligation for the congregation and yet let our priests and ministers merely go through the motions. Who really lets them do that, though? Should we blame the seminaries for poor training? Or the bishops for poor leadership? Certainly in some cases we ought to. But I am convinced that the primary obligation and the only really effective source of change for the better lie elsewhere.

There would be no reason for having people lead us in liturgy were it not for each person's need for regular symbolic plug-in to the mystery of life in God. Those who preside at liturgies can forget that. They can think of themselves as merely appointed by a pastor or bishop to do a job rather than seriously needed by ordinary people who want to come together before God in humility and trust.

Of course, not everyone in a community senses that need with equal urgency. But there is no other place where a minister's call comes from except the general need for someone who can lead us into that holy place where we meet God. The obligation of demanding relevant liturgies, therefore, falls to the persons who know about prayer and want to be gathered with others in prayer that is genuine. It may well be the bishop who makes the demand. (Indeed, the bishop is only our servant, seeing to it that our spiritual needs are met.) But it may also be the widow who sits in the same pew every Sunday at ten and wants more about life's mystery and God's Assurance than about moral obligations, money, or a priest's unprepared thoughts.

How should we go about criticizing liturgies? We should remember that the minister is just as prone to self-assurance and fearful security against the world's uncertainties as we are. For that reason, our criticism ought to be direct, but usually gentle. It does no good at all to withdraw from every incompetent minister as though the entire obligation lay on others' shoulders. But neither does it do any good to blast and pound away at someone for what seems to them like a deep spiritual inadequacy. No matter what the circumstances and the personalities involved, I believe that we must elicit from our ministers the insight that they need to turn to God as much as anybody else. So what if they claim, "I'm no saint." We need ministers who are aware of their inadequacies and fears but who will lead others, fearful like them, to the temple of Assurance.

A liturgy that draws people into the mystery of life in God can be very formal or very informal. On the formal end of the scale, the liturgy that most easily touches the mystery is the funeral. A wedding, on the other hand, is the most difficult. (The other formal liturgies — major feasts, anniversaries, ordinations, and vow-taking — fall in between.) We can see, from our reflections, why this is so. It's not because we prefer sadness to happiness. Rather it's because at a funeral nearly everyone gropes for adequate words to express something about the mystery of life and death. At a wedding, words flow all too rapidly — and are usually about who came, wearing what, and how nice the ceremony is.

The same principle about groping for adequate words applies at the informal end of the scale. I'm thinking of liturgies a celebrant leads for friends in a home or for a group of retreatants. In these liturgies, and in all the more regular Sunday liturgies in a church, the particular facet of life's mystery to be celebrated usually comes out of the readings of the day. Sometimes the point of the readings is obvious; sometimes it is not. It is when the point is too obvious that I get uneasy. The Scriptures are not superficial. The reason we (the congregation as well as the celebrant) ought to take time to prepare for liturgy is to let the readings really speak to a sufficiently deep level of our hearts — to the level, we might say, where we cannot easily find words.

EVEN the words we do find will not be enough. They can only point in a direction and evoke certain feelings about some aspect of the mystery of God's involvement with us. The words of Scripture, the words in the homily, the prescribed words of the ritual, and all the interior words in our hearts, inadequate though they seem, converge upon some particular common wonderment and illuminate its sanctity.

Perhaps there is only one word spoken at liturgy. Perhaps the liturgy is nothing but that single word. God speaks it. And we speak it.

The word is Yes.

God says, "Yes, I am here. Listen to the story of my Son. There is nothing in me that I have not given to him. I have no other Word but him, and I speak that

Word to you. Listen to the story of my People, for in them the Word of my Son resonates and grows in volume and fidelity."

And we say, "Yes, we believe. We bring our bodies to You lined and stooped from caring; we bring our minds to You etched with questions we cannot answer; we bring our hearts to You pounding for more than we know."

To that word all human ambiguity and ambivalence, all the forces of evil and all our unfinished business bows.

FOR the time being, then, before we see clearly the love affair between God and us and welcome it together, we have to count on the fact that we are already in intimate dialogue with him:

> "Is that You? You whom my heart seeks — are You there?"
>
> "Yes," he replies, "I am here. I gave myself to you in the Ancient Day. I am the Spirit of your wonder; I am the true Word in your history. I have never left you."

For this earthly time being, then, we can sing this act of faith:

> "You whom my heart seeks,
> You the ones given:
> The same,
> The same!"